Praise For
Now Waiting

"The reality is that God is good no matter what. But God saying he will do it doesn't mean he will do it in our timing. So what do we do until then? This book challenges us to relish the seasons we are in and to be present in the waiting. Sarah encourages us to shift our perspective from 'God, why aren't you . . .' to 'God, what is it you're doing right now? How can I grow?'"

—**Andi Andrew,** author, speaker, founder of She Is Free, and cofounder of Liberty Church Global

"None of us enjoy the waiting process, and often we are so busy looking ahead that we are frustrated in our current moment. *Now Waiting* is a great book to help us face the tension between where we are and where we want to be. Sarah's writing is practical and real. You will feel as if you have a friend who is cheering you on!"

—**Holly Wagner,** founder of She Rises and Oasis Church, and author of *Find Your Brave*

Now Waiting

Now Waiting

HOPE

FOR TODAY

WHEN ALL

YOU WANT IS

TOMORROW

Sarah Johnson

LEAFWOOD
PUBLISHERS

an imprint of Abilene Christian University Press

NOW WAITING
Hope for Today When All You Want Is Tomorrow

L E A F W O O D
P U B L I S H E R S
an imprint of Abilene Christian University Press

Copyright © 2020 by Sarah Johnson

ISBN 978-1-68426-340-0 | LCCN 2019039907

Printed in the United States of America

LIBRARY OF CONGRESS CATALOGING-IN-PUBLICATION DATA
Names: Johnson, Sarah, 1984- author.
Title: Now waiting : hope for today when all you want is tomorrow / Sarah Johnson.
Description: Abilene, Texas : Leafwood Publishers, an imprint of Abilene
    Christian University Press, 2020.
Identifiers: LCCN 2019039907 | ISBN 9781684263400 (trade paperback)
Subjects: LCSH: Expectation (Psychology)--Religious aspects—Christianity.
    | Waiting (Philosophy) | Trust in God—Christianity.
Classification: LCC BV4647.E93 J64 2020 | DDC 248.4—dc23
LC record available at https://lccn.loc.gov/2019039907

Cover design by ThinkPen Design | Interior text design by Sandy Armstrong, Strong Design

Leafwood Publishers is an imprint of Abilene Christian University Press
ACU Box 29138, Abilene, Texas 79699

1-877-816-4455 | www.leafwoodpublishers.com

20 21 22 23 24 25 / 7 6 5 4 3 2 1

For Grandma Lydia,
a devoted prayer warrior,
faithful servant, and hero in the faith

Contents

Introduction

Life is passing me by. That was my first thought most mornings and my final thought many nights. It felt as though life was happening all around me. My friends and complete strangers were experiencing incredible moments and living out what was in their hearts. And I was sitting on the sidelines, waiting. It's crazy to say such things; I mean, if you look at my life—a wife, a mom of three—it's pretty evident that I'm not sitting on the sidelines. In fact, I actually don't do much sitting these days.

So maybe sitting on the sidelines isn't the best mental picture. Maybe it's more as though I was running in place, like the athlete whose posture shouts, "Put me in, Coach!" I was looking for my opportunity to play, to finally see what was in my heart happen. While running in place, I wasn't able to see the beautiful, vibrant life that God had entrusted me with because I was too busy peeking over at the lives of others. I took their big moments and compared them to my ordinary days. Big mistake. I mean, how unfair is that? And when I wasn't looking at others, I was pointing fingers at myself, because surely I had done something wrong to disqualify myself from God's plan.

Culture is screaming at us to make things happen, to pick ourselves up by our bootstraps, and to be more driven than the rest. It applauds the work of overnight successes and those who get to where they want to go faster. We feel the constant tension of playing catch-up with everyone else. Somehow, they got a jumpstart on this whole thing—they appear to be doing more and working harder. And if you don't figure it out sooner than later, they are going to get what's yours before you have a chance to lace up your running shoes.

If you are waiting for your future husband, everyone around you is getting married. If you are waiting to start a family, everyone is suddenly pregnant. If you are waiting to see your ministry or career aspirations break new ground, everyone is experiencing crazy success. And sometimes others even have the audacity to say, "It just happened."

Even though it seems like people are jumping from mountaintop moment to mountaintop moment, life is filled with hills and valleys no matter who you are. No one is exempt from the unfair, hard, and tough moments. Most of life isn't experienced on the mountaintop but is found while navigating the middle. Chasing the God-sized dream and the promise in your heart looks like many moments and seasons in the waiting as you surrender to his plan, his timing, his way.

I am familiar with the highs and lows that are experienced along the way. I've questioned God's goodness, believed the lie that he has forgotten about me, and doubted the promises he has made to me. I wish I could tell you differently. It hasn't been all doom and gloom, though. My seasons of waiting have also been very encouraging—moments when I was certain that God has had my best interest in mind. Sometimes this paradox of emotions happened within one day.

Maybe today you feel weary or worn down. Perhaps the light has seemed to grow dim with each passing day, and as you look around, it doesn't seem like what you are hoping for will actually happen. Or maybe you are excited about the future God has for you and the promises he has shared with you. And even though you want to experience and walk in those promises today, you understand that some of those things require you to wait.

You're in good company, my friend. You are not alone as you wait. What I have come to find out over the past year as I have shared my story is that everyone is on a journey, navigating the middle, and waiting on God to fulfill his promises—whether it is a marriage to be restored, a baby to deliver, a family member to break free from addiction, a job promotion to gain, or a scholarship to come through. Whatever we're waiting for, it means something to us personally, deep down in our soul. In one moment, we feel so confident that we are going to see whatever it is we are believing for, and in the next moment, we are flooded with doubt and uncertainty. We are faced with this realization that, although we believe, we still have this unbelief that gnaws at our faith, moment by moment.

Here is the good news! Your waiting is not in vain, and what might feel like a wilderness season doesn't have to be dry. It can be filled with joy, power, beauty, and miracles.

There is purpose in your waiting. There is purpose in the middle.

The middle is what this book is all about. It's not about navigating around the waiting season. If you find that book, let me know. But this book centers on how to make the most of your wait. I have not done this perfectly, but there are some things I have learned along the way, whether grudgingly or willingly, that I think will help you while you experience life in the middle. I'm going to share them with you!

My prayer is that when you are finished reading this book, you believe God to be a truth teller and a promise keeper, and you return to your rightful place at his table as his beloved daughter. So what are you waiting for? Let's go for it!

ONE

On Your Mark, Get Set, *Wait*

We live in a social media, digital world where we can see into the lives of people in a matter of seconds—their picture-perfect world compared to ours looks wildly different. We notice results, we compare results, and we are obsessed with results! We place a high value on overnight successes and one-hit wonders and undervalue the grind, the struggle, and the everyday, ordinary choices and the hard work that are necessary to yield the results we wish to achieve. We don't want to know about how long people have waited, or what it took for them to get there. Instead, we want to know the fastest route, and we are hoping, just hoping, they will share their "secret sauce" with us.

Our culture is always looking for ways to do things faster and more efficiently. I am grateful for that, trust me—in the time I did some edits for this book, I simultaneously filled my online grocery shopping cart, ordering my groceries for the week. It took me a total of ten minutes to shop for my family of five. I did not have to get out of my house, put on a decent outfit, or brush my hair. And by the time I finish writing this page, my groceries will arrive at my doorstep. No walking the aisles, no deciding between the gluten-free snack or the kettle chips that have caught my eye more than I'd like to admit. The best part, I didn't have to wait in a single line.

These days, we can have anything we want, whenever we want.

But no matter how hassle-free, quick, and instant the world around us has become, there are things that take time. The promises God has made to you, the purpose on your life, and the destiny you desire to see happen . . . those take time. Just ask any mother after she pees on a stick and finds out she is pregnant. She doesn't immediately start pushing that baby out—she knows that she has ten long months of waiting. If you didn't know this, sorry to burst your bubble. Pregnancy is, in fact, ten months.

Escaping the middle is not reality, but waiting with confidence, certainty, and joy can be! Since we aren't getting out of waiting—honey, we need to prepare for it. Our waiting is our story, so what we do with our times of waiting matters. Crossing the finish line, getting what we are hoping for, or arriving to our destination is what we celebrate and look forward to, but the miracles are found in the waiting. On my journey, I have realized that the good stuff, the best parts of our stories, is in the moments between where we are and where we desire to be.

God has changed my mind about waiting. What I used to push away or resist, I have learned to embrace. I am learning to see my season of waiting not as a punishment or a time of torment, but as a gift from my Heavenly Father who cares about me! He cares so much that he will allow me to wait, to give me the gift of time to grow me, mold me, and prepare me for what he has prepared for me.

The same is for you—God is not withholding something from you to punish you, but he is entrusting you with a season of waiting because he loves you. God is giving you a story to tell—one filled with the miraculous, the moments that matter, the good stuff.

Sidelined

One afternoon when I was picking up my son Jett from preschool, I asked him the same three questions I ask every day: What did you learn? Did you have fun? What was your favorite part of the day? Most of the time, he responds with, "I learned about God." "Yes." "Recess." Sometimes snack time is his favorite; it all depends on what was in the pantry that day. This particular day, he let me know about a story in the Bible that he learned about. I'll give you the story the way he told it to me: "There was a girl named Hannah who wanted a baby. She prayed for a baby, and God gave her the baby. The end."

For those of you who are not familiar with this story, I am sorry—I should have warned you about the spoiler. God gives Hannah a baby. My son did a great job giving me the CliffsNotes of this story. Maybe if I were to have asked you about her story, you would have told it to me the same way. The awesome thing about the stories found in the Bible is that we can find hope in the miracles and in the God-breathed moments others have experienced. At the same time, however, knowing the ending of the story naturally lightens the reality of hardships, the lack, the loss, and the waiting these individuals endured. Knowing that in the end God gives her a baby really makes her time without her promise seem like a breeze, doesn't it?

My husband can watch a movie more than once. It's probably why he can quote many of them. I, on the other hand, cannot. Once I have seen a movie, I don't want to see it again, ever. Unless it's a Christmas movie—in my opinion, Christmas movies can be watched over and over. Once I have experienced the laughter, the sadness, the hardship, and the victory in a movie, it never feels the same the second time through. I already know that he is going to find his daughter or that she is going to save the world. If I do watch it again, I am not nearly as engaged, committed, or hanging on every moment like I was the first time. The same can be true for us when we read stories like Hannah's. We have this bias that it's going to work out. So we aren't nearly as in awe, and we subconsciously disconnect ourselves from the story. Hannah soon becomes a fictional character who, of course, gets the great ending. Hannah becomes another person who doesn't understand our wait.

So, for a moment, I want you to imagine Hannah as your friend or, better yet, put yourself in Hannah's shoes. You are barren, waiting, and as you sit in your waiting, you scroll through the lives of your friends and your family on Instagram, and behold! Another person is pregnant. And you, you are still barren. Year after year, month after month, week after week, and day after day, waiting.

When you take her story personally, you can feel her grief, you can sense her heartbreak, and you can understand her belief. Hannah believed God could, but he hadn't. Have you ever prayed so hard for something, believed God for something, and your reality doesn't seem to reflect that God has even heard your prayers? Maybe you've believed for something for so long that you have come to the conclusion that it's just not going to happen for you.

I have.

Have you ever felt overlooked, forgotten, or pushed to the side by God? That although you have the right heart and are doing all of the right things—feeding the homeless, caring for orphans, serving in church, it's not getting the attention of God? And as you look to your left and to your right, you see everyone else living out and experiencing what you only secretly desire?

I have too.

About twelve years ago, God placed a vision in my heart. It is a big dream, rooted in the belief that my God is a God of the impossible. This dream is so much bigger than me and far beyond anything I could ever accomplish in my own strength. It's been a dream that I haven't been able to shake—at times it has given me great hope and assurance, and at other times, it has brought me so much frustration. Sure, I have seen glimpses and have experienced moments when I felt my life taking big strides toward this God-sized dream, but I know there is more. I know that what God has promised me has not yet come to pass.

I believe God to be true and capable, to be sovereign and omnipotent! I think that is the hardest part for me, actually. It's not about *if* he can, but it's more about if he will do it for me. I have seen him move in the lives of those around me, and I would be lying if I said I didn't often wonder why. Why them and not me? Why has God chosen to give them something and not me? I'm not jealous—I have celebrated and continue to celebrate what God is doing in their lives—but I question whether I have been forgotten, overlooked, or left out.

Maybe you have too.

There is validity to your feelings, but they are not the truth. The truth is, whether it feels like it or not, you are not forgotten or overlooked, and you have not been left out. God knows your name, has a plan for you, and is walking with you. In our waiting, we will be tempted to allow our current realities to dictate what we think, feel, and believe about God. In our waiting, we will have opportunities to discredit his power and embrace a suspicious heart toward him. The enemy of our souls will whisper and roar lies that tell us we have been forgotten, that God is withholding something from us because we don't matter.

But we have a choice in our waiting. We can either believe the lies of an enemy who wants to steal, kill, and destroy our lives, or we can believe the truths about a God who wants to give us life and life more abundantly. And when the truth starts to get muddy, we must look to his Word to be reminded of who he is, who we are, and what he says about us.

So, if you skimmed past the encouragement I was dishing out a few paragraphs ago, here are some God-breathed truths from our Father in heaven.

God knows you and has plans for you:

> "For I know the plans I have for you," says the LORD.
> "They are plans for good and not for disaster, to give you
> a future and a hope." (Jer. 29:11 NLT)

God is working for you.

> And we know that God causes everything to work
> together for the good of those who love God
> and are called according to his purpose for them.
> (Rom. 8:28 NLT)

God has already proven his love for you.

> For God so loved the world, that he gave his only Son,
> that whoever believes in him should not perish but
> have eternal life. (John 3:16)

God is faithful and he will do it.

God will make this happen, for he who calls you is faithful. (1 Thess. 5:24 NLT)

Over the past few years, I have watched others walk into what I have been believing for. When sharing their story, they have innocently and faithfully said things like, "Every time we give God space, he fills it. We've just had faith." In their effort to describe a God who honors the faith of his people, these comments would leave me feeling emptier. I had been giving God space to move, to fill; I possessed the faith and was willing to look foolish, and somehow it didn't seem to move his hand.

So, what did this mean for me? Did I not possess enough faith? Was God punishing me? Had I made some mistake that somehow disqualified me from his plan for me? Were the promises he made me no longer available? Or maybe God didn't trust me? Maybe he didn't love me the way he loved others who were being used by him. Perhaps Hannah wrestled with the same kind of doubts. Since we know that Hannah is not a fictional character of a story but a real woman who believed for a real promise, we can assume that Hannah processed through the same honest questions about God.

When we take our current reality and compare it to the promises we are believing for, it is easy to draw these conclusions and to possess these feelings. God isn't intimidated by our doubts, our fear, or our questions. If we allow them to, these moments can give us the assurance we're looking for from God. When we take our current reality coupled with the questions we have and compare them to God's Word, it becomes evident that God has not forgotten about us. His Word exposes the lies that we don't have enough faith or that we are being punished or that somehow we are disqualified from his plan for us.

The enemy wants to create guilt in our hearts for feeling set aside by God. He wants us to feel badly for our fears or our uncertainties, because he knows that if we yield them to Jesus, our God silences those fears and uncertainties! God not only silences them, but he replaces those fears and uncertainties with more promises that make us stronger, more certain, and filled with more faith. If God isn't afraid of our doubts, we don't need to be afraid to bring them before him. This is the exchange God makes with us.

When we feel we don't possess enough faith, Jesus reminds us, "If you have faith as small as a mustard seed, you can say to this mountain, 'Move from here to there,' and it will move. Nothing will be impossible for you" (Matt. 17:20 NIV).

When we feel we have been disqualified, he reminds us, "What shall we say about such wonderful things as these? If God is for us, who can ever be against us? Since he did not spare even his own Son but gave him up for us all, won't he also give us everything else?" (Rom. 8:31–32 NLT).

When we feel we aren't loved by him, he reminds us, "The LORD your God is in your midst, a mighty one who will save; he will rejoice over you with gladness; he will quiet you by his love; he will exult over you with loud singing" (Zeph. 3:17).

God's Perfect Timing

There is another person who plays a key role in Hannah's story: Samuel, the promise! We could have easily overlooked and brushed past this whole waiting story. We could begin by reading about his story when he is born. But Hannah's story is necessary. And our story of waiting is necessary too. Her story of waiting reveals the nature of God. It reminds us that God is faithful, that he is trustworthy, and that he is good.

There is purpose in her story of waiting, every single part of it. Her desire, her weakness, her pain, her promise to give Samuel back to God, the way she trusted God, and the way God trusted her—all of it. Her tears, her pain, her victory, and her triumph all played a part in history! We get the beautiful opportunity to know the ending of her story, so it can be easy for us to dismiss the in-between, year-after-year, day-after-day reality of her waiting.

We live in a time when we see everyone's highlight reels—the things, the moments, the gifts—but we don't always get the opportunity to witness the process. We see the swaddled baby, the engagement photos, the growing church, the successful business, the published book, and we wonder why. Why is it happening for them and not for us? We compare our reality of waiting with someone else's miracle moment! We dismiss, overlook, and discredit their waiting, when in reality we don't have a single clue what they had to endure or walk through for that miracle.

Anytime I talked about someone else's story, my mom would remind me that I don't really want what they have, and I don't really want to live their life, because with their promise comes their process! There is another woman in this story. Her name is Peninnah. She was Elkanah's other wife, and she gave Elkanah children. So there are two women: Hannah who is barren and Peninnah who is not.

If we looked at the ending of both Peninnah and Hannah's stories and had to pick who we wanted to be, we would, without a doubt, pick Hannah. Hannah became the mother of Samuel, the faithful prophet of God who anointed both Saul and David as kings over Israel. Peninnah, though a mother blessed with children of her own, was exposed as unkind. And that is almost all we know about her. Still, if we looked at these women's lives in the middle, we would be much more likely to pick Peninnah's story. The messy middle parts of Hannah's story, when she waited and longed for God to give her a son, aren't so desirable, especially if you don't know what is waiting at the end. We want the promised miracle from God, but not the process of birthing that miracle.

So, we get frustrated. Frustrated with God for not coming through when we want him to, frustrated with others for receiving what we are believing for, and frustrated with ourselves for believing in this crazy, God-sized dream. But that is why Hannah's story is important! It not only reveals the goodness of God, but also the nature of God, his process, and how he is not a genie in a bottle (resisting the urge to break out my Christina Aguilera impersonation) but a loving Father who cares for us and will bring forth his promises at just the right time.

When I read Hannah's story of waiting, I am all the more excited to rejoice in her "God did it!" story. This is why when we share with others how God has made true on his promise, we must also share our waiting times with them. We must show others how to wait well. I'm not talking about sharing your "woe is me" story on Facebook. I am talking about getting with your girlfriends and sharing what God is teaching you and showing you as you wait. I am talking about letting your guard down and letting people in to see that you don't have it all together, but you remain in the hands of the One who does!

God is not only giving you a promise to possess, but also a story to tell. A story that brings all the glory and all the honor to him! What story will you tell? Will it be one of faith, hope, honor, and glory? I pray it is. Dear daughter of the King, you have been entrusted with the wait, not because God is punishing you, but because he loves you and desires to give you good things! Those things aren't just for you, but they are for a dying world that desperately needs to hear your story of hope and of courage.

It's Not Only about You

We know that Hannah wanted a baby. In the beginning of her story, it tells of her barrenness and her desire for a baby. But in her waiting, Hannah's desire takes on new meaning.

> Hannah was in deep anguish, crying bitterly as she prayed to the LORD. And she made this vow: "O LORD of Heaven's Armies, if you will look upon my sorrow and answer my prayer and give me a son, then I will give him back to you. He will be yours for his entire lifetime, and as a sign that he has been dedicated to the LORD, his hair will never be cut. (1 Sam. 1:10–11 NLT)

Hannah doesn't simply ask for a child to feed and raise, but for a son; she promises to give him back to God to be used by God for a lifetime. We aren't sure about the kind of prayers Hannah declared in times before, but it doesn't seem like this prayer was the same. This prayer is when everything changes.

At this moment, she does something we don't see any other woman do in the Bible—she goes to pray for something specific and something personal. And in this prayer, she makes a vow that if God will give her this promise, she in turn will give her son back to God. In the same moment she is pleading with God to give her something that she desperately wants, she promises to relinquish full control of it. Her season of waiting developed within her a desire for more than a baby to swaddle but a promise to deliver.

Can I tell you that the promise you are waiting for is not just for you? Your promise is for others too. God didn't just give her a child, although that would have been sufficient, but he entrusted her with a Samuel. God had a plan for Samuel, and he knew that he had to be born to a trusted mother like Hannah. God knew that Hannah would keep her word, because he saw that she believed God would keep his word to her.

It's never been about if God can give you the thing you are waiting for, but a matter of when. When are we willing to, in the same breath of our asking and in our waiting, relinquish full control, giving God full access to use our promise for his purposes? Being that Hannah is my soul sister, I am almost certain her desire for a baby wasn't always to give her child back to God. I am sure she longed for days to hold her baby, to be a part of every milestone, and to have her baby in tote to bring before God, year after year. But, in her waiting, Hannah became the person God needed her to be in order to deliver the promise he had for her.

Who we are becoming is more important to God than where he is taking us and what he is giving us. He can give us that desired thing, right here and right now. But he hasn't yet, so that tells me he is making us more ready, giving us more time to embrace the story he is writing for us. It reassures me that waiting is important and valuable, because there is purpose in it.

But while we are waiting on our journey from here to there, we are faced with a real enemy who tries to fill our minds with lies, every single day. Imagine for a moment going to worship and sacrifice to the Lord knowing that, in that atmosphere, you were going to be greeted with torment. Not just once in a while, but as often as Hannah went to the house of the Lord, she was provoked by this other woman. "And her rival used to provoke her grievously to irritate her, because the Lord had closed her womb. So it went on year by year. As often as she went up to the house of the Lord, she used to provoke her" (1 Sam. 1:6–7).

In 1 Samuel, it doesn't say that Peninnah bothered Hannah because she was more beautiful than Peninnah was, which I could almost guarantee Hannah was, because mean ain't pretty! No, Scripture says that Peninnah would irritate Hannah because of her barrenness. It also says that even though Peninnah gave Elkanah children, he loved Hannah more. He loved Hannah so much that every year when he would offer up a sacrifice at Shiloh, he would share out the portions of meat and give Hannah a double portion, which probably added fire to Peninnah's jealousy toward Hannah and caused Peninnah to taunt Hannah even more.

Hannah's label of barrenness was her most vulnerable place, her weakest place. Something she had to face every day, and especially when each woman would get a portion according to her children. Peninnah targeted Hannah's weakest place. Though we don't have sister wives lurking around our house (if you do, I will have to write a book about that on another day), we do have a real enemy who targets us.

The enemy of our soul attacks the vulnerable places in our lives, the places we are trusting God in the most audacious, ridiculous ways. Like Hannah, who is barren and believing God will give her a child, we are believing for God-sized miracles. And that makes the enemy mad—oh, it makes him really mad. Mad that we would even for a moment place our faith and our hope in God. That we would dare to believe that God can and that he will. It makes the enemy squirm to think that in our barrenness, we would continue year after year, day after day to come before the Lord in worship. So he attacks us, he irritates us, and he provokes us.

Why?

Because our place of weakness is our place of promise. If he can defeat us, he can keep us from coming back year after year to go before our God yet again and asking and believing for our promise. The enemy is not worried about what we have experienced but about what we have yet to see God do in our lives. What I love most about Hannah's story is that we never read about her addressing this other woman. It doesn't say that she told her to back off or gave the town some good material for a reality TV show. She doesn't mention her rival in any of her prayers. Instead, Hannah goes to God, year after year. As Peninnah rolls up in her minivan with all her little blessings, Hannah arrives there alone. And although it plagues Hannah greatly, it doesn't keep her from going to God again.

Friend, there is a real enemy who wants to disqualify you, set you back, and break you down. He is targeting your weakness; but rest assured, your place of weakness is also your place of promise. And although the enemy targets you, you are marked by God, and no weapon formed against you shall prosper.

Don't allow the lies of the enemy to keep you from going to God, again and again.

God Is Good

God is good! is a churchy saying we hear all the time. It's fun to say when I've found the perfect parking spot or when things have gone my way. But there was a time I couldn't stir up enough courage to declare this as truth for me. Sure, I believed that God was good, but I wasn't fully convinced that he was good to me.

I remember attending a women's conference, sitting about two rows away from the stage, when the worship team sang a song I had never heard. Over and over the lyrics declared the goodness of God. From the top of my lungs, I declared that God is good . . . until it came to the point in the song that declared he's never going to let me down. As the room of women began shouting this powerful truth, I stood in silence.

I couldn't do it. I couldn't find the bravery to say such things.

Did I believe God is good? Yes! Did I believe he was good to me? I wasn't sure.

I have experienced disappointment, hardship, and trials. I have watched friends lose their children and their marriages. I have had prayers that I feel go unanswered and things not turn out the way I desired. I stood there as tears began to form a puddle on the floor underneath me, wanting to say those words, but not being able to.

I placed my hand over my heart, once again, and as I did, I looked over and my best friend looked right in my eyes and said, "He's not going to let you down." I searched my soul, my heart, and my thoughts, and as I began to take to him the pain, the hurt, and the moments when I have felt let down, I began to see that although I have experienced these things, he *hasn't* let me down. Although things hadn't turned out the way I wanted them to, he wasn't the author of my pain. He wasn't the reason for my letdown. Instead, he was the one who, every time, took my broken pieces and made something beautiful. He was my comfort when I felt shattered, my healer when I experienced pain, my provider when I felt uncertainty, and my ever-present help in time of need.

He has never let me down, and he isn't going to let me down.

If I'm transparent, friend, it's still a little hard to type these words. But I know that just like anything else, I have to develop my faith muscles to believe this as truth. Maybe you feel like I do. You believe that he is good, but you aren't convinced that he is good to you. Can I whisper something to you today? He's never going to let you down.

Will you experience hardship? Yes.

Will you experience heartbreak? Yes.

Will he use all things for your good? Yes.

I have kept this song on repeat in my car, and every time I find my hand over my heart, and each time I say it, I believe it more and more. I have listened to it so many times since then that my kids have it stuck in their heads! When I begin to shrink back, hold back, or rethink this bold declaration, they begin belting it out. Their childlike faith brings out the best in my faith and I sing along with them. Because this song is true: he is good, he is good to me, and he's never going to let me down. He is good, he is good to you, and he's never going to let you down. He is not the author of your pain, but the One who took your pain to the cross. He is not bringing pain on your life, but will use your pain for his glory.

He is not punishing you. He is not keeping something from you as you wait.

I am sure Hannah had her moments. Moments she saw the faithfulness of God happening all around her, except toward her. Times when she saw the goodness of God being lived out in others, but not for her. I am certain there were times Hannah believed God was good, but that he wasn't good to her. In her story, we never read about God speaking to her. Not one single time. The only time we see anything close is when Eli tells her that God has heard her. Keep in mind, that promise came moments after he mocked her and accused her of being drunk. There was a lot of silence from God. It's during the silent seasons and moments in our waiting that we can become the most suspicious of him and his actions toward us.

This moment is when it all matters, the one when our hearts could become bitter and our light could grow dim. This moment, when we feel forsaken by God as Jesus did, and far from him. When his promise seems to serve as a horrible reminder that God isn't moving on our behalf. We must receive his perfect love that casts out all fear. We must remember that he is good and that he is good to us, that he causes all things to work together for our good. That is the God we serve.

Not only do we have to remember who God is, but we must remember who we are to him: his daughters.

There's Room for You

Before I attended my first writer's conference, I participated in a preconference webinar that provided me with some insight about the weekend and how to prepare. Attending this conference was a dream of mine, something I circled for a few years. God provided every detail, proving to me it was exactly where I needed to be and that he was with me all the way.

The webinar was so insightful and helpful for me in so many ways, but I will never forget this one statement the woman leading the discussion made to each of the anxious, unsure, excited aspiring authors tuning in.

"God does not divide. He multiplies!"

She was silencing the fear of every girl that the other girls in the room were their competition. She was disempowering the lie that if God was doing it for others, it meant there was little left for us. This was a breakthrough moment for me. I believe it can be for you too. Let me say it one more time for the girl in the back who skimmed past that line!

"God does not divide. He multiplies!"

What does that mean for you? It means that her victory doesn't mean your failure. It means her miracle doesn't have to be your misery. It means that you serve a God of more than enough, not a God of just enough.

God's desire for us is that we live big. He is a God who is more than enough, and when he begins to bless others, let it serve as a reminder to you that he is able. When the waves of blessing and abundance mark the shores of the lives of others, remember that it's the same tide that brings in the things you long for, believe for, and are working hard for.

The way we approach God in prayer and the thoughts we think reflect our view about him. This is why we must remind ourselves daily about the goodness of God. When we keep his goodness front and center, our posture changes. We begin to see him as a promise keeper and a truth teller, approaching our void and lack in a new way. We are not beggars asking for crumbs; we are his daughters and he is a good Father. What he has is not running out, and what belongs to you will not pass you by. As daughters, we have access to all the good things he has.

As women, we wear many hats and carry out different responsibilities. We are business owners, stay-at-home moms, wives, students, creative thinkers, writers, freedom fighters, athletes, and teachers. Each one of us is serving our community in a unique capacity. What we do with our lives and how we spend our days often shape our view of the world and ourselves. And many times, what we are waiting for is also interwoven with who we want to be—whether that is to be a mom, a wife, a writer, or a decorated athlete. When who we want to be takes precedence over who we already are, we begin to respond from a place of lack rather than a place of abundance, a place of confidence.

So, as you wait on your promise to be a wife, mother, teacher, CEO, or any role you hope for, remember that you will always be a daughter of God. That alone is enough assurance that God has not forgotten about you, he has not overlooked your situation, and he is madly in love with you! Yes, we are mothers, friends, entrepreneurs, teachers, and students all desiring to contribute to our communities differently, but we are also God's daughters who are loved uniquely. Daughter—loved, valued, and created by a loving Father. And although you may do many things and desire to become many things, you are always a daughter of the King.

TWO

Win the *Middle*

When my girls were in first grade, they both received a certificate for making honor roll. I think honor roll for first grade is kind of silly, but that's beside the point. They did a great job in school, and my husband and I wanted to honor them for their hard work. When we received their honor roll certificates, we made it a big deal. Did the "hooray, we are proud of you"—the whole thing. We even promised them a new gift! Well, of course, it wasn't a gift I was going to buy right then. In fact, we knew it would be a couple of days before we made the trip to the store. I'm sure you can already tell me the rest of the story, right? They asked for that gift every single moment. Every time we loaded up in the car, got dressed, or looked their way, they wanted to know if it was time.

I couldn't take the asking any longer and did what any good mother would do: I promised them that we were going to get the surprise . . . tomorrow. I know, it must have felt like eternity for these two. But tomorrow was the soonest I could get there, so tomorrow it was. The next day, we decided not only to get the surprise, but we also thought it would be awesome to make a fun day out of it. Time together and shopping for a new surprise sounded like the perfect day. It did for my husband and me, anyway.

From the rising of the sun, we were bombarded with questions: Where are we going? What are we doing? Are we going now? The questions wouldn't relent. Each time, however, we reassured them that we were going to have a day filled with surprises. We found a cute donut shop close by where you could eat fifteen of them because they were so cute and bite-sized. This place served yummy coffee, so we ate and sipped our coffee. After that, we journeyed to a beautiful park that overlooked the water. The Florida fall weather was divine, and we were kissed with the perfect amount of sunshine.

As fun and memorable as this morning out was for us as a family, it was practically torture for our daughters. They didn't really experience any of those exciting moments. They did and yet they didn't, all at the same time. Because although we were experiencing incredible things together, we hadn't arrived to their desired destination. We hadn't arrived at the toy store, which was all that was front and center in their minds. No matter how many times we assured them that we would get there, they couldn't settle into that understanding and embrace all the moments in between.

I second-guessed my decision to let them in on the surprise. Maybe I shouldn't have told them anything about a surprise and just given them some high-fives. Perhaps if I did that, they would have savored every delicious bite of those donuts. Rather than hurrying us along, they would have paused a little longer to enjoy the reflection the sun made on the water as we walked along the bay.

As we were walking back to the car, I looked over at my husband and said, "You know this is totally us, right? You know that when God gives us a promise, something really exciting to look forward to, all we can do is focus on that thing. So much so that everything else is a little less exciting. The incredible, savory, fun things that we are given along the way to our promise seem more like a burden and a detour than the cherry on top." Sure, we could have started the day with the surprise and then gone out for donuts, but I wanted my kids to know it's not just the desired destination that matters, but everything else along the way. That, and Momma wanted donuts and coffee before she could be generous and buy Legos. And all the mommas said, *"Amen!"*

God is not making us wait because he is punishing us, even though it feels like that a lot of the time. He is not withholding something from us, but entrusting us with a story. A story that includes others, a story that displays his glory. A story about his faithfulness in the midst of pain, a story about his leading in the darkest times of our lives. A story about his goodness despite what our reality looks like.

We can get so caught up in the destination that we miss all that he is doing in our lives.

And if most of our lives is spent on the way to a desired destination, we must learn how to fully embrace the other gifts, even when it's hard. Rather than seeing them as prolonging our wait, let's view them as necessary moments that are preparing us, growing us, and sometimes freeing us.

Quickest Route

I loved living in Los Angeles. It has beautiful beaches, diverse people, chic boutiques, fun coffee shops, and lots of traffic. Just kidding, the traffic is what I liked least about living there. No matter what time of the day it is, there is always traffic. If you need to drive twenty miles to your destination, plan for your journey to take you at least an hour. I remember the first time we down-loaded a navigation app to our phones. Did I just date myself? Unlike previous navigation tools, this app was unique because it had been designed to navigate you around traffic. I remember how cool that feature was at the time. I also remember being equally skeptical to use it, considering that the routes it often suggested seemed bizarre.

After a fun outing with friends one afternoon, we hopped in our car, and before hitting the road, we plugged our destination into our trusted navigation app, in hopes it would give us the fastest route home. Then, we started our trek home. Our friends in the other car decided to follow along behind us. Once we got into familiar territory, we were surprised to see the app directing us to go a different route, a route we had never taken home before. Rather than fighting against it, we took the suggested route and continued on our journey. We quickly noticed that our friends who had been behind us weren't following us anymore. At this point in our journey, they knew the way home and took the route they were most familiar with.

Well, guess what? We arrived home more than thirty min-utes before our friends. We promise we didn't speed! During that drive, we questioned many of the directional choices the app was encouraging us to make, because the majority of the time it didn't feel like we were making any progress. When we arrived home before our friends, my husband looked at me and jokingly said, "Her ways are not our ways!" It made me laugh because it sounded a lot like a Bible verse I've heard many times before: "'For my thoughts are not your thoughts, neither are your ways my ways,' declares the LORD" (Isa. 55:8 NIV).

God is a trusted leader who is capable of leading us and guiding us. He is sovereign and knows every twist and turn, roadblock, and traffic jam that is on the road ahead. He knows the best route for you and for me. All we have to do is trust his leading. But trusting God isn't always easy, whether we find ourselves in familiar or unfamiliar territory. Especially when where he leads you doesn't look like the quickest route.

It is rather entertaining when we travel with others because they have their own traveling preferences and share their own ideas of which route is truly the best. Can you imagine traveling with over one million other sojourners? The children of Israel were on their way to the promised land, and Scripture states that God purposefully led them through the middle of the wilderness. It is like when you hop on a plane to travel south, only to have your layover in a state north of you. This journey that should have taken them forty days took them forty years. It wasn't the result of a more affordable ticket but of following the voice of God through their leader, Moses. There was a quicker route, but God didn't lead them that way. He led them to a longer route, one that required time in dry, desert lands. Not because he was punishing them, but because he was rescuing them and setting them free.

So they set their sights on the promised land with enthusiasm, just like many of us do when we first set sail. I'm sure they experienced the same nerves that you and I do when we are about to begin a new adventure, whether it's a new job, moving to a new location, starting a family, or getting married. In the beginning, we have a list written out of the many things we are looking forward to most, hardly ever including moments of resistance, hardship, or difficulty.

The children of Israel were focused on their final destination, while God was focused on who they were becoming. More than setting them physically free, he wanted to set them spiritually and mentally free. The children of Israel had endured years of bondage, and they were in desperate need of rescuing. But the way we understand or interpret rescuing isn't always how God chooses to rescue us. God could have taken them the quickest route, picking them up and dropping them off in the promised land. But God's rescue led them through the wilderness.

Their enthusiasm was not long-lasting as they experienced crisis and times of testing, but we read that in each of these moments of hardship and lack, God's goodness was ever-present.

Can you imagine being able to tell the story of how God parted the Red Sea or how he showered carbs from heaven to feed you? Looking in and looking back on their story, we see the evidence that the presence of God was near. Yet we don't read about their wonder at the miracles they experienced firsthand, but instead we read about their utter discouragement and frustration. Rather than seeing God providing for them by sending manna from the sky, they begged God to send them back to slavery. They kicked and screamed, groaned and complained, not about what God did but in how he chose to do it. In every turn and plot twist, we see why the wilderness was necessary for their growth and for their freedom. The lessons learned and the miracles they witnessed all point to why God chose this kind of rescuing, a plan to help them learn how much they needed him.

No matter the journey or the journeyer, no one who is growing or choosing to move forward is exempt from this process. This motley crew tallying over a million had only known slavery and bondage. And while it is easy to presume that anything outside of Egypt would have been better than the life they knew, the Egyptian way of life, although dysfunctional, was comforting to them. It was familiar territory that made them feel safe. We might not be slaves to an earthly master, but there are ways of thinking, relationships, habits, and patterns that make us feel safe though they are dysfunctional and unhealthy. And we sometimes beg to go back when we are experiencing things we don't feel are necessary.

Being a writer, I am sure it is easy to guess what my favorite subjects in school have always been. I loved English, writing, communication classes, and anything that required writing or speaking words. Math and science, not so much. If I had a nickel for every time I asked, "When am I ever going to use this in real life?" I would own a vacation home in Hawaii. I knew I wasn't going to be a scientist or do anything that required me to say Please Excuse My Dear Aunt Sally when solving a math problem that required order of operations. I can with confidence say to you that I have never had to use that specific knowledge since. But the time spent working through math problems taught me to push through mental barriers, use strategies, and think differently—all tools for my toolbox of life.

We often feel the same way about a problem or an experience we find ourselves standing in the middle of. We ask, "Why do I need to go through this?" and "Why is this necessary?" Some might say, "Everything happens for a reason," or "God works in mysterious ways." But I am saying, "God uses everything for our good!" Everything we walk through, experience, and endure can be used for good in our lives. Everything, and I mean *everything*, that the children of Israel learned was a valuable lesson that could only be learned in the wilderness. But the wilderness looked nothing like their promised land, making it difficult to see the goodness and purpose of God. The middle hardly ever looks like where we are going.

We live in a developing city. It is charming, with both the big city and small town vibes. It seems like new development is going up every day. One particular afternoon, I noticed a piece of land that had once been home to tall trees stretching as far as the eye could see now blanketed with dirt. I pulled over and got out of my car and began to walk the grounds. It looked barren, desolate, lacking growth or sign of new life. I pressed my heels into the ground, closed my eyes, and stood there for a few seconds. This middle is a confusing place. What was is no longer, yet what will be doesn't seem possible. In the middle, we are faced with the many opportunities to lose faith in the process. From my vantage point, it looked like this development was taking steps backward. I mean, at least there were tall trees and some sort of life before, right?

Until I opened my eyes and looked out. About a hundred yards from where my heels remained sunk in the dirt, I saw builders, tractors, supplies, and signs that read Building Something Beautiful. Builders step foot on the same ground and consider it progress. The middle is where builders keep moving forward, knowing they are one step closer to building something beautiful.

God is our maker, and he is building something beautiful. He is on the ground of our middle, and he is not intimidated or insecure by what he sees. We might see digression, but God sees progression, knowing that in every step we take forward, we are growing into who he has called us to be. He sees the big picture and loves us too much to allow us to charge ahead ill-prepared. Sometimes it is hard to imagine a good God being so close and so near in times of great trouble. But as we read the story of the Israelites, we see that God was and is a very present God: "By day the LORD went ahead of them . . . and by night" (Exod. 13:21 NIV).

God has never nor will he ever leave us. He is close and he is near, providing for us every step of the way.

I'm All In

In my circle of close friends, I have been known as the Jesus girl who believes God audaciously. I am the girl you can count on to pray with you, cheer you on, and remind you of God's promises. I have witnessed up close the miracles and the incredible things God can do when we simply trust him. At the same time, I have also experienced doubt and walked through seasons when I wavered in my belief. I don't think any of us go through life unscathed by the realities of our situations or avoid seasons when our faith is tested. Moments when what we see looks wildly different than what God has promised us. Moments when we have to ask ourselves, "Even in this, do I still believe? "In the middle of this, am I fully convinced?"

One day, as I was journaling and spending some time alone, I penned these questions in my journal.

"Am I fully convinced?"

"Am I fully convinced that *God is able* to do what he promised me?" This was a pivotal season of my life, a time when I was getting ready to take steps into uncharted territory. I took my belief in one hand and my unbelief in another, and I laid them before God. Sifting through my fears, doubts, insecurities, excitement, and anticipation, what remained was a resolve in my heart that I was fully convinced. Here was my response:

> I *am fully convinced.* I am convinced that it has little to
> do with my efforts and everything to do with my Jesus,
> my Father, who loves me, who cares so much about
> me, and who has already gone ahead of me. No matter

the outcome, he is faithful. No matter the answer, he is good. No matter what, I know that everything he has promised will happen, in his timing, in his way.

This is a girl who finally gets it. A girl who has surrendered her dreams back over to the One who gave them to her. A girl who fully believes that Jesus is really for her, and that his plans will happen in her life.

It's one thing to have hopes that something God has promised you could happen, but it's another thing to possess the assurance that it actually will. Being fully convinced is risky. When we take this position, we can appear to be naive or as though we are not in tune with reality. Think of old Abraham and his barren wife Sarah, who were going around telling people that God promised them a child—and they actually believed it! Perhaps we'd think they were a little crazy. For those who know the full story, it's easy to brush past the facts and overlook how crazy it was for them to believe, because we know that God made true on his promise.

But if we place ourselves in their middle moment—the moment between when their promise was given to them and when they finally gave birth to Isaac—we begin to see their fully convinced, fully assured belief as risky.

What if what they truly believe for doesn't happen?

Nothing in their life or about their reality screamed, "We are going to be parents!" Perhaps many of us can relate to that. Nothing in our life resembles or even hints at the promises God has made to us. The ground looks barren, the resources are dry, and there is no movement signaling a change in weather. Whether it's about our health, our relationships, our finances, or about the children we've been promised to raise, when we take inventory and assess the situation, we can become discouraged and lose hope. But, friend, here's what I am learning: our realities don't disqualify our faith; they make room for our faith. A faith that is not rooted in our current situation, diagnosis, dream, or even promise, but in our God who moves and does some of his best work in situations that look utterly impossible.

Being fully convinced means that even when I don't see it, I will not take my eyes off the One who is able.

Being fully convinced means that even when I don't feel it, I will not allow my heart to drift away from the One who holds the promise.

Being fully convinced means that even when things seem to be combating against or pushing back on the progress or growth to my promise, I will not allow it to weaken my position. I will continue to believe that God will do what he has said he will do.

Abraham is credited with being a man who was fully convinced.

However, if you know their story, you also know that Abraham and Sarah didn't navigate their waiting season perfectly. One time, Abraham lied to people about who Sarah was to him, claiming she was his sister. Sarah was the first person to LOL (laugh out loud) at an angel when he first brought word that she would be a mom. And Sarah even convinced Abraham to sleep with their maidservant in efforts to make it happen.

Yet, in all of that, they are still credited with possessing a faith worth noting. I'm grateful for God's grace, which is always enough even when I don't get it right. When I experience doubt, when I literally or figuratively laugh out loud at the promises God has made me because my reality tells a wildly different story, or when I utterly mess up and take matters into my own hands, God's grace is sufficient. His grace reminds me that it's so much more about him than it is about me; and even though I can feel pretty powerful, I am not powerful enough to thwart God's plan. Instead, he shows up, continues to remain faithful, and chooses to involve me in his beautiful plan.

It encourages me to know that the fulfillment of the promise isn't all on me getting it right. The promise is that even when I mess up, fall short, or lack experience or resources, he is enough and capable. Our inability doesn't disqualify us. I wonder what kind of new reality we would see and experience if we took the same position. I'm not suggesting it would speed up the process of our waiting or even change the outcome; however, I firmly believe it would change the way we see things in the here and now.

Being fully convinced gives us new lenses in which to view our current situation, seeing the possibilities instead of the lack. With a new position, we see the seemingly small and insignificant moments as gestures from heaven, reminding us that he is in the waiting.

Being fully convinced in what seems impossible is daring, risky, and bold—and it's an incredible new way to experience the adventure that is found from here to there.

Abraham was fully convinced that God was able to fulfill his promise.

In the same way, I am fully convinced that God is able to fulfill his promises to me. I am fully convinced that the Author and Finisher of my faith is a beautiful storyteller; and I am fully convinced he wants to tell a great story through my life. A story that displays his goodness.

· · · · · · · · · ·～· · · · · · · · ·

THREE

Run Your *Race*

My daughter Kennedi has a dream to become a well-known ballerina. Since she was itty bitty, she has worn tutus and ballet slippers, jumping and twirling everywhere she goes. When she was six, we put her in dance for the first time. It was so much fun watching her take her first steps toward her dream. She worked hard at learning all the movements, listened closely to her dance instructor, and was so expectant for her first ballet recital. The recital was perfect in every way. In a room filled with dancers of all ages performing incredible dance numbers, I only had eyes for one girl—that was my Kennedi.

Months later, Kennedi and I were lying in my bed one night talking about our dreams. She began sharing with me the details of the vision in her heart. "Mommy, I see red curtains that go from the floor to the top of the ceiling. I see beautiful red seats, a crowded room, a black stage, and a pretty backdrop that matches the theme of the performance." She continued talking about what she was wearing and provided me every last detail.

And then she said these words in the most honest, yet slightly disappointed tone: "But sometimes your dreams look like an old, dusty coffee shop!"

I think I almost spit the water out of my mouth. I knew exactly what she was referencing. The hall where her first dance recital was held was not the prettiest venue. Looking at it, I would have to agree with Kennedi and say it looked and felt like an old, dusty coffee shop. My eyes welled up with tears, because that truth hit home with me. I affirmed her statement, letting her know that yes, sometimes our dreams look like an old, dusty coffee shop. Sometimes our dreams and what we are believing for look nothing like what we see in our hearts. Being the intuitive little gal that she is, she asked me, "Is this your dream?"

We shared a moment of silence as our dreams came front and center to our minds and hearts. I looked back over at her and answered. "This moment today has everything to do with my dream, but it's not the final number in this adventure. That old, dusty coffee shop isn't your dream, but it has everything to do with your dream. And while it might have felt old and dusty and looked nothing like what you see in your heart, it's meaningful and beautiful." Although we often see our dreams as a distant place, person, or promotion, in fact, we are standing in the midst of our dream. It might not be fully developed, but where you are right now is still a part of your story.

Your old, dusty coffee-shop-looking recital hall is not wasted space but holy ground. A place you have been planted, purposed, and fashioned. It is shaping ground designed to help you develop, grow, and become ready for all that is ahead for you. It is a place of abundance and miracles, purpose and promise. But if we aren't careful, we can spend too many days wishing for shinier days and not fully capturing the beauty of our today. If Kennedi chooses to pursue her dream of becoming a ballerina and one day finds her feet on a stage that looks like the dream she so eloquently described, it will be because of many ordinary days endured and delighted in.

As her mom, I'm leaning in and soaking up every single moment. I watch the recitals when not a single girl is doing the same movement at the same time and wonder if the random freestyle-looking movements were part of the dance number or if they lost track of where they were in the song. In a room full of dancers, my eyes are always glued on my girl because every step and moment matters to me.

I think this is how God feels about us. He is leaning in with pride and adoration for his kids, watching us grow and learn to dance the number he's entrusted us with, on the stage he's positioned us on. His eyes are glued on us because he knows that every step and moment matters. He is just as present and invested and interested in our old, dusty coffee shop recital as he is when we are performing in *The Nutcracker*. One is not more valuable or meaningful than the other. I know I can't recover the days spent overlooking the ordinary days, the days wishing I were somewhere else, doing something different, but I can grab hold of right here and right now, choosing to see the adventure that is today!

Friends, let us grab hold of what today has for us. Let us see the wide-open space not as barren land but as opportunity, knowing that the process to produce a harvest takes many ordinary days, many days of faithfulness, and many days of showing up.

These are the good old days! These are the days that shape our stories.

When I hear people share their story, they almost always talk about the good old days. The days when they had very little or when what was in their hearts was just a dream. They share about the difficult seasons with such care and gentleness, almost as if they miss those days. I can picture Kennedi sharing about her dancing experience and looking back on this old, dusty coffee shop as something special. I don't want to rush past the moments that I dread in my present situation, hoping for better days. I want to speak about and cherish these small beginnings in the same way I will one day. Because these are the good old days, right here and right now.

I Will Not Compare

Meaningful and beautiful quickly turn old and dusty when we compare our first dance recital to someone else's *Nutcracker* debut.

We hear it time and time again that comparison is the thief of joy, yet we fall into the trap time and time again. I wish I didn't feel compelled to write this, and I wish I could say that I have silenced this lie once and for all, but I haven't. Are we still comparing our lives to someone else's? Haven't we heard a dozen sermons warning us against it? Have we not read a bazillion blogs supported by Scripture and personal stories of how devaluing it is? Have we not scrolled through at least ten catchy captions attached to someone's incredible Instagram-worthy photo reminding us not to compare their moment with ours? Yet here we are.

It's a big fat trap that we can clearly see standing in the way of others but blindly walk into ourselves, each time surrendering to all of its divisive side effects that leave us stranded. We can't help but notice all the vibrant moments in the lives of others. Compared to our lives, their experiences make ours seem dim. It's unfair to us, it's unfair to the people we are sizing up our lives against, and it's unfair to God. We pray for and desire a unique story until God gives us a unique story. When it looks like we are falling behind or coming up short, we want to exchange this unique story with something a little more familiar and safe. What we want now overwhelms and takes center stage to what we want most.

My three kids have been raised in the same house, by the same parents. Two of them even shared the same womb for nine months and have pretty much lived the same life, every day. But they are not the same and neither is my love for them. My husband, BJ, and I love and nurture their hearts, passions, and interests uniquely. Oftentimes, in our best effort not to dish out this cookie-cutter love on them, the way we honor and nurture them as individuals often feels like we are leaving another one out or overlooking the other.

That couldn't be further from the truth.

They don't want to be loved the same; but sometimes the same feels more comforting. Sometimes the same feels good. Do you ever feel like this? You find yourself praying and desperately wanting a unique, unlike-anyone-else kind of story, purpose, and vision; yet, secretly you desire the same story as someone else? Let me encourage you the same way I encourage my kids. Heck, let me encourage myself! You don't want the same, and even though it feels comforting in the moment, your story is so unique, so beautiful, that it doesn't deserve to be compared to anyone else's.

In Hannah's prayer to God, we don't see a mention of Peninnah's name—not once. Even though Hannah saw God grant someone else children, she didn't ask for that woman's story. She never said, "Hey, God, do for me what you did for her!" But, instead, she asks that God would remember her request. If Hannah had asked for Peninnah's story, she would have gotten a

Peninnah story! And although that would have felt good in the moment—to be a mother, just like Peninnah—she may not have been the mother of Samuel, someone devoted to God.

We never hear the names of Peninnah's children, and we only know of her as being someone who pestered Hannah. Hannah is known for waiting on God, for trusting God, and for seeing God make true on his word. We know her as someone who was chosen to be the mother of Samuel. Imagine if she had fallen into the trap of comparison, and rather than standing on her promise, she was busy asking for the same story as someone else. Hannah is a great example for us who are waiting. Although we can see that God can fulfill our desire because he has done it for someone else, we are not going to allow our waiting to convince us to settle for someone else's story.

God wants to love you, uniquely! So let him! Allow him to gift you, show you, and lead you in a personal way. When you really pause and reflect, you know that you don't really want the same as somebody else. God sees you, and you matter to him. He has not overlooked you nor forgotten about you. Instead, he has plans, dreams, gifts, and moments crafted just for you with your name on them! Embrace your story, be fully present with a grateful heart toward your Heavenly Father, knowing that he doesn't love you the same, but he loves you uniquely.

When we see the Christian life as being about getting and receiving rather than about giving and surrendering, we fall prey to comparison. We become frustrated with our lives and resent the very things that God has entrusted to us. We feel shorted and overlooked by God and by others.

I actually care about people, actually love God, and actually walk in integrity! Those words came spewing out of my mouth one day (on many occasions, actually), even though it's hard to admit. I had been doing all of the right things and everything God had asked me to do, yet none of it seemed to be bringing me closer to my desired destination. As I looked to my left and my right, it seemed as though everyone else, including a few whom I didn't think were as deserving, were walking in what I was still believing for.

Sometimes when we discuss comparison, we address the obvious: she has something, I want it, and it makes me sad or frustrated not to have it. But the kind of comparison I'm thinking of is subtle. This form of comparison is dressed up in *righteousness* but so deeply rooted in *pride*. Somehow, I felt deserving of a reward because of my obedience. Somehow, I had earned my spot in the fulfillment of the promises God had made to me. I not only had the audacity to bring all of my "good" deeds before God, but I also carelessly made harsh and unjust judgments about other people. Somewhere along the way, pride knocked on the door of my heart, and I not only opened it, but I let it set up camp.

Have you heard of the story about the Pharisees who brought a woman caught in adultery before Jesus? Being the Pharisees they were, they confronted Jesus with a question, hoping to trick him. And Jesus being Jesus, he didn't give them the answer they were hoping for. He wrote something in the sand for all to read. Except us! I know, what a cliffhanger. Many have suggested what it might have been that Jesus wrote in the sand that day; but whatever it was, it caused every single one of her accusers to turn away and leave.

GIFs are my favorite things to use in text messages. If I had to pick one for this scripture, it would be a person eating popcorn with eyes wide open watching this moment transpire. It has always had me leaning on the edge of my seat to watch Jesus silence the accusers. This passage has always made me so glad to be on Team Jesus, and anytime I have read this portion of Scripture, I have always taken note of the grace of Jesus and the audacity of those Pharisees. But guess who isn't eating popcorn and watching this episode as though it doesn't have anything to do with her? This girl right here. Instead, I am very aware that this scripture has everything to do with me, making me keenly aware of the stones in my hand.

I see that I am not any more deserving of mercy than those on my right or my left. I am a sinner who has been saved by grace, who messes up time and time again, and who desperately needs the grace and mercy of the Father every single day. Nothing I have done in the name of Jesus grants me VIP access to his promises. And what God chooses to do in the lives of others is none of my business. Right here and right now, I choose to drop the stones that I have tightly gripped in my hands. As I dare to size myself up with those around me, I am confronted by the truth that God doesn't need my input about anything or anyone. No, this is not righteousness; this is pride. This attitude doesn't reflect a heart hidden in the love of Jesus but reveals that this heart isn't ready for what I think I so deserve.

I don't feel as bad saying that I struggle with comparison. But comparison is a shiny word for jealousy and envy, two words that don't flow off the tongue so easily. Jealousy is "I want what you have, whether that's position or possession." Envy is "I don't want you to have that, whether I get it or not." Envy and jealousy are a direct attack against you and all that God wants to do in your life. It is a vicious cycle from which we need to be delivered. This is so much more than addressing the moments when you wish you could take more Instagram-worthy photos of you and your kids sipping tea and eating biscuits in bed, wearing matching pajamas to be more of a social media influencer like her. Envy and jealousy deserve no room in our hearts, and eradicating them is more difficult than a catchy Pinterest quote that tells us, "Comparison is the thief of joy" that we all like and then go on our merry little way.

I've heard people say they unfollow people on social media because they feel *tempted* to compare. They go on to say how freeing and positive it has been for them. I see their intentions here, and I'll be the first to admit I've done this too. However, we don't need to unfollow everybody with more money, a better-looking house, a larger church, or more followers on Instagram. We need to deal with our hearts. Sure, you might not need to be bombarded with their beautiful, shiny, social media-worthy life every single day, but unfollowing them doesn't help you overcome comparison. Unfollowing them helps you avoid the envy that is rooted in your heart. And no matter how many people you unfollow, envy will rule your life whether you're on social media or not.

Remove social media from the equation completely, and jealousy, envy, and comparison are still just as real. Long before there was a place online to examine the lives of others, there was a real enemy who was always looking for ways to convince us that we were being treated unfairly by God. Whether I am pouring three glasses of milk, handing out handfuls of candy, or serving up scoops of ice cream, my kids always, and I mean always, compare their portion to the portion of the other two. Most of the time, their complaint comes before a thank you is ever uttered. It usually sounds like this: "Mom, how come he gets to have *all* of that, and I *only* get to have this?"

Notice the emphasis on the two words *all* and *only*. Maybe you're more worried about the extra calories that come with two extra pieces of candy, so the sibling squabble doesn't hit home for you. But maybe you and your spouse have been working overtime, taking on extra projects, getting your credit in line, saving, making sacrifices, and waiting for all the details to come together to buy your first home. Then your friend texts you letting you know that a beautiful home practically landed in their lap! Is your first response that of comparison? Do you immediately compare their *all* to your *only*?

When my kids were little and first starting to play the comparison game, I would practically measure out three even cups of milk, count out the exact number of candies, and try to make sure all the scoops looked the exact same size. Until one day I just responded, "Yep, you're right! She did get one more piece of candy than you did, and guess what? That is okay! Sometimes your sister is going to get more of something, and sometimes you will too, and it's okay!" I quickly realized that always trying to make it fair wasn't really fair at all. We've heard people say a million times, "Life isn't fair." That is true; life isn't always fair. Sometimes people will get more than we do, and that is okay! Do we want less? No. But are we able to celebrate when they get more without feeling like we've been left out?

Knowing the nature of God is critical here. God knows what is best for us—so much so that he will allow us to wait, sometimes what feels like a lifetime more than others. Sometimes it looks like we are being entrusted or gifted with less than our brothers and sisters on this journey. And sometimes it will feel completely unfair. That is why we must remind ourselves of who God is, knowing that he has never nor will he ever withhold something from us with the purpose of putting us down or keeping us out.

Instead, when God allows us to experience the waiting or the withholding, we can rest assured that he's got this whole thing under control. He knows our desires, and he takes great pleasure in giving us the desires of our hearts. And just as I believe that to be true, I also believe that his perfect love knows exactly what I need. This isn't a cliché moment, when we just nod our heads at the statement we feel we have to believe and walk away still offended by God or suspicious of his actions toward us. This is a moment to truly examine what we believe to be true about God. This is a moment to lean in and unpack the layers of hurt, disappointment, and misunderstanding. This is a moment to sift through the rhetoric and get to the truth of the matter and ask ourselves the hard questions.

Do we believe that God's nature is always good to us?

Do we believe that he is for us?

Do we believe that he cares about what concerns us?

When we are standing in the waiting, and each step toward healing, restoration, and reconciliation feels like we are walking in the mud, do we feel punished by God or positioned by him?

When we know who God is, we will see that the waiting isn't a punishment but that we've been positioned right where we are for a purpose. When we notice that others are experiencing a miracle moment, we won't assume it's because God loves them more. Instead, it will cause our faith to be strengthened, believing that if he did it for them, he can do it for us.

When we walk through uncharted territory and feel like we've been abandoned by God, knowing who he is and what we are to him will serve as a compass, reminding us that he will never leave us. Knowing the true nature and character of God shields us from the darts of the enemy so that when comparison tries to knock on the doors of our hearts and minds, we can, with confidence, resist the temptation to believe anything different than what God has revealed.

Hear me clearly: this is not a moment where I am casting stones at you. I am standing with you in the crowd, and together we are deciding to drop our stones one at a time. I am uncovering the lie that says comparison is par for the course and is something to deal with because we live in an Instagram world. I am helping us see the truth about what envy does to us personally and to those around us. It pollutes our hearts and divides our communities.

People are going to get what you are praying for. Others will experience what you desperately believe God for. Those around you, whether complete strangers or your BFFs, will possess what you are working so hard to achieve. And because we know we can't unfollow everybody, how do we combat this temptation to be jealous?

Communion

I grew up in a church where we did communion the first Sunday of every month. It was my favorite Sunday because, well, snacks. I am all about snacks! Sometimes, when my parents weren't looking, I would reach in for two crackers, even though they didn't taste all that good. I went through the motions of it all and hoped the pastor or leader chosen to do the ceremony would cut right to the chase. Sometimes I didn't even wait for the prayer to commence before eating the bite-sized cracker.

Years later, the same would be true. Maybe I wouldn't reach in for two crackers, and I would display a little more self-control and wait for the prayer to finish before partaking in the cracker and the juice. And while I am thankful for these faith communities, and for the opportunities they created for me to remember what Jesus did for me, it wasn't until recently that I realized this wasn't supposed to be a tradition for elders to remind their pastors to do only on the first Sunday of the month. It's something Jesus instructed us to do often.

Before Jesus went to the cross, he ate with his disciples. As he broke bread and drank wine with them, he gave them clear instructions to do this in remembrance of him. When I think about the timing of this, knowing that Jesus's time on earth was nearing its end, what he chose to do with his time carries more significance. The early church understood this significance and followed Jesus's instructions to share communion as an opportunity to remember the sacrifice Jesus made.

Communion is about remembering what Jesus did for us; and when we do this often, it sifts the envy out of our hearts. We remind ourselves of the life that he freed us from and the sin that enslaved us, including envy. We remember that envy and jealousy have no place in the heart of a child of God. Communion is not only about us remembering what Jesus did; it also gives us an opportunity to come before him once again, to lay down our lives once again—our dreams, our hearts' desires, our victories, and our brokenness. It helps us identify areas where our hearts have drifted away from the truth of who he is and exposes areas where we have not trusted him completely.

Communion is about each other. Communion is to be done at a table, in our churches, and in our communities. Communion connects our hearts to one another. We see that we are a part of the family of God. We recognize that the same God who freed us has freed our brother and sister to our left and to our right. Without rival, without envy, without jealousy. Communion cultivates gratitude for each other instead of puffing ourselves up above one another. When our posture is surrendered at the foot of the cross, we know that no one is above another and that we aren't more deserving of anything. The same blood that washed away our sins is the same blood that covered everyone who believes in the name of Jesus!

This is why we should take communion often.

Serving

Anytime my husband and I are heading out the door on a date, we go down the list of things—we remind our kids of the house expectations and give our babysitter the scoop. No matter how long or short the list is, we always leave the most important instructions for last. We have realized no one is really paying attention, so whatever she hears last is what she is most likely to remember.

And Jesus did something similar when he chose to wash the feet of his disciples during the Last Supper. Jesus could have done this ceremony during the three years he walked with the disciples, but he chose to share this moment with them in the Upper Room the night before he was killed. He stood up from the table and began to wash the feet of his disciples, one by one, washing their dirty, filthy feet with water and drying them with his garment. During that day, and maybe even today in our culture, foot washing was among the lowliest of positions, and here was the King of kings, purposefully and intentionally placing himself right there.

This moment was a foreshadowing of what he would soon endure on the cross, and it addressed a very present issue the disciples were dealing with. Guess what that was? Comparison! Right in front of Jesus, right in the middle of this moment, his disciples started comparing themselves to one another. But this didn't catch Jesus off guard. This is his reply:

"Rather, let the greatest among you become as the youngest, and the leader as one who serves. For who is the greater, one who reclines at table or one who serves? Is it not the one who reclines at table? But I am among you as the one who serves" (Luke 22:26–27).

Serving realigns our hearts. Serving is an antidote to envy. Serving doesn't allow us to think of ourselves as better than anyone else. Jesus was the Son of God, yet he chose to be born in a dirty barn, to live as a carpenter, and, in that moment, to wash the dirty feet of men who messed up daily. When you feel envy and jealousy creep into your heart and attempt to take center stage in your actions, serve someone!

Go and Tell!

When was the last time you shared your story with someone new? Not the story of how you got the cute pair of shoes you've been eyeing on sale or how you got the front-row parking spot during your last trip to Target. When was the last time you shared your redemption story? The story of when Jesus rescued you, forgave you, and set you free to live your best life. Sharing our stories combats envy and jealousy.

For about a year, it seemed like everyone I knew was posting pictures or videos of themselves or their kids using the hashtag #LivingMyBestLife. These pictures were usually taken at Disney World, at the beach, or doing something fun and entertaining. During one of the darkest moments in my waiting journey, I remember lying in my bed with a pillow over my head. I was crying out to God, unable to get out of bed because my heart felt so broken. That particular year, we experienced a lot of hard moments. We witnessed friends get divorced and walked alongside friends who had lost children. It seemed like every day we received news that we didn't want to hear or experienced situations that we were hoping would turn out differently. I was tired, I was frustrated, and I was so upset.

This time, I was comparing myself to others by declaring how much better they were than I was. *I wasn't cut out for this. I didn't have what it took.* I was convinced that I somehow had disqualified us from the promise, that I had royally messed up this whole thing somewhere along the way. I went through every decision, and they all led me back to feeling unqualified. I was ready to give my letter of resignation.

As others were #LivingTheirBestLives, I was experiencing what felt like hell on earth. I was lonely, defeated, hopeless, and over it all. I shared my heart and I poured it all out to him. I told him that I was upset when he didn't heal my friends' son; I was heartbroken that he allowed our other friends to lose their son unexpectedly. I shared with him that I felt responsible for our friends who went through a divorce. I told him I felt like a failure.

I'm so glad God can handle our honesty. Right in the middle of me raising my fists to God, he met me there. He comforted me with his love, he reminded me that he is God and I am not, and he showed that his love for me and for all my friends was put on display when he sent Jesus to die on a cross. I was reminded of the first time I received this overwhelming grace and acceptance by him, a day that marked my life forever. When I accepted Jesus as my Lord and Savior, I was saying yes to a life surrendered to him.

Our story of when we accepted the truth about Jesus reminds us of what this life here on earth is all about. That's why we have to go and find others and tell them. Because although we might experience some #LivingOurBestLife moments, we will also experience some gut-wrenching, hard moments too, often at the same time others are experiencing their mountaintop moments. And while every blessing and miracle God does in and through our lives serves as hope for what we are believing for, nothing compares to what Jesus did for us on the cross! Our day-to-day and the exciting, new moments we experience can make our moment of salvation seem like a distant memory.

In that dark moment, I had to come to an understanding that I was okay and fully grateful for the cross. And if God never did anything else for me, if he never answered another prayer request, and if he never gave me what I believe he has promised me, I would still serve him with all that I am. Perhaps you need to remind yourself of your redemption story. Perhaps you need to go and find someone in your life and confess and declare how God rescued you. God doesn't owe us anything. If he never does anything else for you, would that be enough?

Celebrate

I have made it my personal ambition to be the most encouraging person, to be the cheerleader for my friends or strangers as they wait on God, to believe for the audacious and do incredible things in his name. I want to be the first clapper, the girl who will look you in the eyes and tell you how incredible you are, how awesome it is going to be, and that you've got what it takes. When a door opens for me, I don't want to grip tightly to whatever it is alone but grab another girl by the hand and look around to see who I can take along with me.

I want to be a safe place where others can let down their guards, share and dream, and unapologetically run the race they've been called to run. When an opportunity comes my way, I want to look for who else can share in that blessing. No more hoarding, no more worrying, no more suspicion of those around me. Along the way, I have disarmed the lie that says if they win, I lose out on the celebration. I've been celebrating the victories and miracles that happen in the lives of others. I've been embracing the truth that if God could do it for them, he could do it for me! It may not be in the same way, or in the same timing, but seeing his power revealed in their lives no longer brings me hopelessness. It fills me with great hope.

We were meant to live free! If you have found yourself striving, chasing, hiding, and hoarding, here's your invitation back to his table, as his daughter. Get rid of the insecurity that has made your life small, rid of the hopelessness that has clouded your heart, and rid of the idea that you don't belong at his table. It breaks my heart that many of God's daughters are looking for their place at his table of belonging too. Just like a child who doesn't know what constant, unconditional, reckless love looks like and feels like, who doesn't know abundance but lives in a reality of lack and scarcity, can hesitantly journey through this life afraid of what is around the bend, so can we when we are unaware of who we are!

I have never experienced lack. Even in the toughest of times, when my husband and I would sell spaghetti dinners to local businesses so that we could have money to pay our rent, God has always been faithful. And as I look back on all that he has brought me through, I know that he is still faithful. Yet I have wavered in my belief. I have trusted him with my eternal salvation, yet experienced doubt because what I see looks nothing like what he has promised me.

Fear says hold on tight. Faith says give it away.

Fear says if I share, I'll lose out. Faith says whatever I need, he will supply.

God's plan for us is not to live life with our hands closed shut, holding on to what we have in fear of coming up short. Instead, life is meant to be lived with our hands, arms, and hearts wide open and giving generously with a true understanding that all we have has been given to us by a generous God who gives good gifts.

* * * * * * * * * * * * * * * * *

FOUR

But I Want It *Now!*

I waited in line for almost five hours for cinnamon rolls once. Adding the word *almost* makes me feel a little better about it, honestly. Have you ever heard of cinnamon? Ha, just kidding. These sweet, gooey, calorie-punching rolls are baked fresh every day at a family-owned farm in Florida. For years, people from all over have visited this farm to get a taste of the goodness. We were weeks away from moving out of South Florida and decided to take a trip to see what all the hype was about. To be specific, this farm was over an hour away, and after doing a little research and asking our friends about it, we decided to make the trek early. We willingly woke up before six o'clock, loaded up the kids in the car, and drove over an hour away.

Our hope was to get some cinnamon rolls, buy a few other treats at the farm, and maybe even do some strawberry picking. We had it all planned out—this was going to be a fun outing together with the family and some friends who were up for the adventure too. Everyone else must have had the same friends, because as we arrived, we were greeted by what felt like the entire town who was already setting up camp. We couldn't believe our eyes; the line was wrapped around the entire farm. My mouth watered at the thought of those rolls. Surely, they have to be the best cinnamon rolls in all the land for so many people to willingly spend their Saturday morning, many with kids in tow, standing in the beating sun. My kids looked really confused, but they didn't dare ask any questions. They saw the excitement in my eyes and carried on.

After about an hour, I started doubting this decision, but as I looked around at my husband and our friends, I knew we were committed to the process. As we were chatting, one of the owners of the farm came around and started yelling out numbers. He came by us and said, "FOUR!" At first I thought he was getting ready to take us to the front, like they do at a theme park when they need a single rider. That wasn't it. He was giving us our wait time, and four was the number of hours we had until we would meet the cinnamon rolls from heaven itself. I kind of coughed and almost passed out. The way he did it baffled me, actually. He didn't say it like, "Hey, only four hours, guys, stay with it!" This was more like, "Here is your sentence; may the odds be ever in your favor." No one budged, no one turned away, no one left. Not even the guys who were about a hundred yards behind us, waiting in the FIVE section. We are not quitters, we told ourselves, and we remained in line for four hours.

For a little reassurance and without wanting to appear too nosy, we subtly peeked into the boxes of cinnamon rolls as those who had gone before us returned to their cars. Their grins said, "Victory!" giving us just the encouragement we needed to endure.

After telling each other our whole life stories, including all the pets we ever owned (there is a lot you can cover in four hours, just saying), it was finally our turn. Being a part of the FOUR team, it seemed silly to buy only one. One dozen, that is. And even though they were bigger than our heads, we bought enough cinnamon rolls to feed a small city.

We looked around for seating or a fun place to enjoy the rolls and the scenery, only to find one park bench in the distance. Looking to my left and my right, I quickly realized there wasn't anything else to do beyond buying these rolls, so our plans to have a fun fall afternoon out on the farm had now been reduced to finding a place to sit while we ate. Without any calorie judgment toward one another, we gathered around the park bench and took our first bite. We brought out the dramatics, repeating over and over how delicious these things were, trying our best to channel the inner victory grin we'd seen all morning long. Our victory lasted all of about three and a half minutes, until we all got real with each other. These weren't the best cinnamon rolls of the land. In fact, I couldn't tell these rolls from the ones I make straight out of the can on Christmas morning. Okay, maybe that is a little dramatic, but I'm getting a little fired up recounting this story.

You know how our parents recount the time when they had to walk to school in the snow for miles? Well, I am now the parent who can recount the time she willingly waited in line for almost five hours for cinnamon rolls. I can without any hesitation tell you we will not be back to the farm anytime soon. But that's not because it was a horrible experience. That's because I have a grocery store within a mile of my house. As I think back on the hours spent there, I cannot recall a single bitter or frustrated person. In fact, everyone was happy and optimistic as they waited. Why? Because it was very clear what they were waiting for and how long they were going to have to wait to get it. It was clear and it was known, with no room to complain or be upset. And while I am not trying to draw a literal parallel with what you are waiting for and my story of the cinnamon rolls, I think we can learn something here.

You and I experience the most frustration when we place unfair expectations on our waiting season.

I experienced frustration when I discovered that there weren't any fun fall activities to partake in. No one told me there would be entertainment; I just assumed there would be. So I created a whole experience in my mind, only to be frustrated when what I thought was going to happen didn't actually happen. I was underwhelmed when the cinnamon rolls I waited in line for weren't the best in all the land. Guess what? Not one person told me these cinnamon rolls were the best in all the land; I just assumed they would be.

My expectations weren't unrealistic. There could have been some fun fall activities to enjoy on the farm, and these babies could have been the best in the land. Bringing it home to our stories of waiting, the same is true. The times I have felt the most frustrated have been when I placed unfair expectations about how and what was going to happen, only to be let down when it didn't happen that way. Scripture says, "Many are the plans in the mind of a man, but it is the purpose of the LORD that will stand" (Prov. 19:21). This verse is frustrating, isn't it? If you're anything like me, understanding that we aren't as in control as we think we are is a tough pill to swallow.

I am sure you've heard the saying, "If you want to make God laugh, tell him your plans." I understand the idea of this statement, but I don't believe this perspective reflects the nature or the goodness of God. Anytime I have heard this line, I have pictured a sarcastic tone of laughter, as though God is sitting on a big throne in heaven laughing at us. God doesn't laugh at his children, and he is certainly not trying to prove us wrong. He is a good Father who loves us so much that he listens to the deep cries of our hearts, and considers our earnest desires and well-thought-out plans with care. In love, he takes our cries, our desires, and our grandest plans and gives them purpose. He isn't the critic who mocks your biggest dreams, most audacious prayers, or detailed plans. He isn't sarcastically laughing at you as you pour your heart out to him.

Frustration comes in and begins to set up camp in our hearts and minds, shifting our perspective about God and about our situation. We begin to see the goodness of God through the lens of our frustration, leaving us feeling like the joke is on us. It feels like somehow God is squandering our dreams and is no longer interested in the promise we are waiting for. The enemy of our souls desperately wants us to think this way. He wants us to allow frustration to guide our thoughts, emotions, and actions, leading us to the conclusion that our steps of obedience have led us to a dead end.

Think about the Garden of Eden and the encounter Eve had with the serpent. Before that infamous conversation, Eve had everything. She knew no insecurity, hardship, or lack and walked with God in total freedom. The goodness of God was all around her. What an experience that must have been! But when the serpent arrived on the scene, he had a plan to convince her to doubt God and be suspicious of his intentions toward her. With one question, Eve no longer saw God's goodness in all that he had given to her, but she now saw God's goodness through what he wasn't allowing her to touch.

When we see God's goodness through our current situation, it is going to leave us frustrated. We must fight to see our situation through the goodness of God. How different would the story have gone if Eve had seen the goodness of God all around her, rather than seeing that God was withholding something from her. A lot of people like to blame Eve for her moment of weakness, myself included. I can count at least two times, both in the context of childbirth. Thank you, Eve. Thanks a lot. But I know that I have made similar decisions time and time again when I have allowed frustration to rule my emotions.

Back to the cinnamon rolls.

The owner of the farm was very specific about how long we were going to have to wait in line. He was equally specific about how this was our decision to stand in the beating sun for the length of time he called out as he passed by. There wasn't anything we could do to make the line move faster, there weren't any fast passes like they have in Disney World, and Uber Eats wasn't taking any pickup orders. The only thing we were responsible for and in control of was *how* we waited.

I wish I could tell you how long your season of waiting is going to be or how it is all going to play out, but I can't. I also wish God was more like the farm owner, walking by us and yelling out the time it will take to see our dreams happen. But he doesn't. He doesn't keep us guessing to bring stress, anxiety, and discouragement to our lives. And while I would like him to give me a date on my calendar that I can highlight and plan a Thank the Lord My Wait Is Finally Over! party, my understanding and belief in his goodness give me the confidence I need while I wait. It isn't a one-time *aha* moment when I actually believe God to be good, but this is something I have to remind myself of over and over again. It is a daily decision to take my fears, my distrust, my anxiety, and my grief to God. I choose to see my waiting through his goodness, every day.

Instead of waiting in confidence, I have been like the person standing in line at the grocery store who is tapping her feet, checking her watch, and huffing and puffing while demanding another cash register be opened because I have been waiting too long. I have allowed frustration to rule my heart and to cloud my judgment, leaving me feeling like God was laughing at my plans and mocking my effort.

So, how do we wait in confidence when God doesn't give us specifics?

Shifting Our Perspective

Let's go back to the scripture that made us a tad bit frustrated a few pages ago: "Many are the plans in the mind of a man, but it is the purpose of the LORD that will stand" (Prov. 19:21).

I like the beginning and I like the end of this scripture. But the big ole *but* that connects these two statements is what makes it go down like watered coffee. And who wants watered-down coffee? Speaking of coffee, let's pretend you and I were sitting together drinking coffee, and as you were sharing your frustrations with me, I leaned over to you, placed my hand on your shoulder, looked you in the eyes, and said, "Friend, don't you worry. God's purpose is going to stand!" I am sure that although it might not fix your situation, it would change your posture. You would stand shoulders back, chin raised as you were reminded of this beautiful truth.

Imagine we were having the same conversation, and I leaned over to you as you shared your frustrations, and I said, "I hear you, *but* it's God's purpose that is going to stand." That statement might not feel as encouraging. You might feel like I was taking something away from you, or that I was giving you some bad news. It all comes down to that big ole *but* (pun intended) and the perspective in which you receive it.

In Scripture, we see the two words "but God" time and time again:

> As for you, you meant evil against me, but God meant it for good, to bring it about that many people should be kept alive, as they are today. (Gen. 50:20)

> My flesh and my heart may fail, but God is the strength of my heart and my portion forever. (Ps. 73:26)

> And when they had carried out all that was written of him, they took him down from the tree and laid him in a tomb. But God raised him from the dead. (Acts 13:29–30)

As we read these verses, we are encouraged by these two words: *but God*. When Joseph's brothers did evil toward him, God intervened and turned it for good. When David's heart and flesh failed him, God intervened and his strength was sufficient. When Jesus was killed and laid in a tomb, dead, God intervened and raised him from the dead! These two words shout "Victory!" and send adrenaline into our bodies. When God intervenes, it's always a good thing. When our lives are hidden in Christ, no matter the situation, there is always a *but God* that turns whatever we are facing to work in our favor.

Our situations are not the end of the story when our lives are surrendered to Jesus.

The same is true when these two words interject the understanding that although we have a five-year plan drafted up in our prayer journals and calendars, God's purpose will stand! It is always a good thing when God has a say-so! It is uncomfortable, and it is not always easy to embrace, but if we are compelled to shout "Victory!" when we rejoice in the truth that God raised Christ from the dead, then we can also rejoice in the truth that God loves us too much to allow things to go according to our plan.

I used to celebrate and thank God for the open doors and the answered prayers. But, more and more, I have learned to celebrate the closed doors and the prayers that were not answered according to my preferences. I have learned to be more grateful for the moments when my prayers that God would use my life and make my life meaningful caused a *but God* moment in my life. When he took my heart's desire, my most audacious prayer, and all my details and made them meaningful.

I don't dare try to say that I celebrate the times when I was praying and believing God for a miracle and the healing never came. Those have been gut-wrenching moments that didn't go the way I wanted them to. I have walked alongside friends who have lost their spouse, their children. I have seen people navigate brutal divorce firsthand, and I have had friends not receive their healing of cancer on this side of eternity. Every time, I desperately desired a *but God* moment for the healing to come and for the breakthrough to happen. Our hearts long to be with our loved ones who have passed, and for those who have lost their marriages, *but God*! Even in death, we have victory. Even when we thought we knew how something was going to go, and in spite of our deepest cry for healing and restoration, when Jesus died and was laid in that tomb, it was not the end of that story, *but God* raised him from the grave, defeating death, hell, and the grave!

There is always a *but God*, and it is always, always a good thing. When we choose to see his intervention, frustration has no room to fester.

No More Striving!

I have always been a with-it person, the go-to gal who can get the job done. I believe God has made me this way. My parents, teachers, and mentors helped cultivate this type of work ethic in me over the course of my life, and I am grateful for it. If you are familiar with the StrengthsFinder test, my top strength is achiever. If you are not familiar with the StrengthsFinder test, it is an assessment that helps you discover and define your strengths. Achievers like me work hard and take great satisfaction from being productive.

It is very natural for me to take the same approach when it comes to following Jesus. It also makes waiting a very frustrating process for me. I see a goal, or an assignment, and I am ready to get the job done. A plus B should equal C. Right? If there is a problem, I want to fix it. If God has entrusted me with something, I want to leverage everything to make the most of this investment. I will build a team, share the vision, and go and do what I have to do.

The achiever in me has enabled me to lead groups, influence organizations, and oversee projects, yielding success in many areas in my life. The achiever in me has also been my worst enemy. I have been the most frustrated when I have approached situations like a project to be completed or a task to be achieved. Rather than viewing this life as a calling, I have approached it like a job. When you work a job, you do what is required of you and you get a paycheck. But a calling is not a job, and the exchange we make with God is not like one we make with an employer.

I believe God created me with the strengths of an achiever, but that does not mean he is asking me to strive or make something happen all on my own. He is only asking me to be faithful. My attention was so laser-focused on results that I forgot the results aren't always up to me. Giving all of my attention to my desired result, without even realizing it, I had taken my eyes off Jesus.

Frustration stews when you and I make an idol out of our assignment or the promise we are waiting for. It is our responsibility to be faithful; it is God's responsibility to make the promise fruitful. Jesus encourages us, "Seek first the kingdom of God and his righteousness, and all these things will be added to you" (Matt. 6:33). We stew in frustration when our focus is not on God and his righteousness, but on ourselves. When we work as if it all depended on our efforts alone, and when those efforts don't seem to be making progress or impact, we will be frustrated.

No, this isn't to suggest that we can sit on our hands and wish things into existence. Being faithful doesn't mean not working hard. Being faithful means doing our part and believing that God is going to do his part. For the goal-setting girl, keep setting those goals. For the girl who loves her to-do list, keep with your organizational skills. For the person who is an achiever, keep working hard. But, in all these things, keep your attention on Jesus!

Shifting Focus

As I was driving to work one day and my speed reached just over sixty miles per hour, my steering wheel started to shake. Not in a dangerous way, but just enough to get my attention. It wouldn't shake at fifty-nine miles per hour or under, but the moment I crossed over to sixty miles per hour, the steering wheel would begin to shake. Let's just say it took me a little longer to get to work that day.

We called our trusted mechanic, and he let us know to bring it into the shop the following day so he could check our car's alignment. Sure enough, it was our car's alignment that needed to be adjusted. Whether you bump a curb, experience an accident, or just use your car daily, over time your car needs to be realigned. Although it's a minor shift, it can be dangerous to drive a car that is out of alignment.

The same is true for us. Our day-to-day experiences and demands put a lot of focus on our efforts and relying on ourselves to get things done. Sometimes small bumps along the way cause us to unknowingly take our focus off of Jesus and transfer it to our situations, causing us to live life out of alignment. So when frustration rattles our day, we must check in with ourselves and once again realign our focus. We must daily remind ourselves that God is God and we are not. We must daily remind ourselves that he is the One who has the ability to make it happen.

Perhaps what you are waiting for isn't a place or position, and your frustration isn't rooted in your inability to achieve a desired result; it's the result of your inability to change a situation. Maybe you desire to have a child, or you are believing for healing in your body. The understanding that you are not in control is frustrating. In the same breath, acknowledging the reality that you are not in control can shift your perspective off you and back on to Jesus, the Author and Finisher of your faith.

When you seek God, you are reminded of his character, his goodness, his strength, and his faithfulness. When you seek God, you can confidently remind your situation that God is bigger. When you seek God, he reminds you that he has you front and center. This understanding cultivates a deep-rooted assurance that he has a plan for you, and that assurance changes everything. You have not been left in this season; you have been planted right where you are—to bear fruit, to grow, and to bring you closer to what's in your heart. Today more than ever, I believe that you are exactly where he wants you to be.

Chasing God

God is the dream-giver, he is the promise-maker, and he is the truth-teller. So, let's make sure we are chasing after him, not after dreams and promises alone.

How do we know the difference? Our dreams shout, "Look what I have done!" Chasing after him shouts, "Look what he has done!" Chasing the promise looks like striving. Chasing the Promiser looks like abiding. In our waiting, we have to constantly reevaluate where we have placed our focus.

One summer, BJ and I had the chance to get away for a few days. It was a beautiful, much-needed time away from the day-to-day responsibilities. One morning, we decided to take a little dip in the ocean. We were talking and sitting in silence, taking in our surroundings and soaking in the sun. After a little while, we decided to head back to shore. Until we noticed we weren't anywhere near where we had first ventured into the waters. Over the past hour or so, we had drifted along the shore. We were a long way off, and our chairs that were once in plain sight were now very hard to see. While we were carried off in conversation, the waves and the current carried us away from where we had begun. We had no intentions of moving away from our part of the beach. Our intentions were to stay close. But we drifted, and before we knew it, we were far from where we began.

The same can be true for our lives. If we are not intentional about abiding in and keeping our eyes fixed on the Promiser instead of the promise itself, if we forget that we are not called to a single vocation or life goal, but that we are called wholly to follow Jesus, then we will find ourselves far from where we began.

I know you are a with-it girl, and I am sure you can get any job done, whatever it is. You are smart, resourceful, generous, and wise. Throw that kind of drive into a culture that promotes success and doing it all like it depends on you, and you are revved up to get the ball rolling on this promise that you've been given. You are ready and have it all mapped out, knowing exactly how you are getting from where you are to where God has promised you will be. And while God has uniquely created you and given you talents and gifts beyond measure, he is not asking you to make it happen. Chasing God does require effort on your part, but it doesn't all depend on you.

In the process of moving from where you are to where you desire to be, there will be many opportunities for you to take your focus off Jesus and place it on yourself. Many moments when you will be tempted to take the reins and get it done, no matter who is coming with you. But when we do this, we begin to move away from a posture of abiding into a place of striving. We aren't the heroes of our stories, and God isn't asking us to make it happen. God is the hero of our story, and he simply asks us to live our life worthy of the calling on our life. Yes, we will be active and faithful with what he has entrusted us with. It also means stepping into uncharted territory as we continue to follow his leading.

That is more than work ethic or determination, friend. That is a life hidden in Jesus, focusing on and running after him. It doesn't say strive, it doesn't say hustle, it doesn't say grind it out. When we do it like it all depends on us, we are left frustrated. I heard someone say the secret to her success was that she worked harder than everyone else. That might sell a few tickets to her success seminar, but the statement is terribly misguided. I do believe in hard work, and I do believe that if you want to be a good steward of your gifts and talents, then you must be actively growing and working hard. But hard work doesn't guarantee you success, nor does it earn us a better place in God's kingdom. He tells us to lay our lives down, not build them up.

Chasing our promises will take us to places we never desired to go and to places God never intended for us to be. Remember Abraham and Sarah (called Abram and Sarai before God gave them new names)? God gave them the promise of descendants, but they got antsy and started chasing it on their own. Sarai was a smart gal and started to look at her situation; they were old and she was barren. If this promise was going to come to pass, she needed to figure out how to make it work, right? Her servant Hagar got pregnant by Abram, which only made matters worse. Now Abram had a son with Sarai's servant, and Sarai didn't want anything to do with Hagar or that baby, so she kicked them out of the house.

I wish I had been a fly on the wall that day. Sarai thought this plan was a good idea, until it wasn't. Rather than waiting on God, they allowed impatience to rule their hearts. Seeing their reality more clearly than the possibility caused them to work outside of God's plan for them.

This story serves as a strong reminder not to get ahead of God, but to remain focused on him. When we lose sight of Jesus and begin taking things into our own hands, we will make decisions that do not reflect God's plan for us or for others.

Our season of waiting does not exclude us from making decisions. At every turn, we will be given opportunities to take control or to trust God. Will we focus on the reality of our day, or will we be led by the Spirit and choose to see what is not yet? Before making these decisions, we must first evaluate where we have secured our confidence. If our confidence is hidden in ourselves and in our own ability, then we will be tempted to get the job done on our own. If our confidence is rooted in the approval of others, we will be tempted to explain our obedience or downplay what we know to be true. Not wanting to look foolish in front of others, we will look for a different route.

Where have you secured your confidence? Is it in the reality of your today, in the approval of others, or in the track record of how things always seem to go? Has your confidence been centered around you and your efforts, forcing things to happen and taking actions that God has never asked you to take? We might not intentionally be placing our confidence in ourselves, but the weight of our waiting can cause us to. So how do we keep our focus on Jesus? How do we ensure we don't lose sight of the Promiser in pursuit of the promise?

Abiding

"If you abide in me, and my words abide in you, ask whatever you wish, and it will be done for you" (John 15:7). We like the end of this verse! We can have whatever we want. It is as if God himself is our personal assistant, ready to grant us everything we have ever dreamed up, right? Not quite. The latter part of this verse is contingent on the first part. *If, then. If* you abide in Jesus and you allow his Word to abide in you, *then* what you wish for and hope for will align with his will for you.

Spending time with the Lord has a way of quieting our anxious hearts. Ridding our minds of fear and doubt, he calms our restlessness and breathes confidence and assurance over us. When we abide in him, he reassures us of the promises he has made to us, and he removes the expectations, time frames, and parameters we have added to what he has said to us. When we abide in him, we are made aware of the idols we built in pursuit of his promise, and we once again give him the place of authority over all of it.

Here's the thing. God is already working out what you are worried about, and the miracle you are believing for is already on its way. So why do we pray? We pray because it's our communication with heaven. When we do, God reveals his plan to us. Not every step and usually not every detail, but he reassures us of the value we are to him. When we pray for his will, our hearts begin to reflect his heart. When our hearts reflect his heart, our words begin to declare his truths. When our words echo the will of heaven, our prayers become prophetic declarations, no longer saturated in pride, fear, or worry, but now hidden in truth!

When we release the prophetic declarations, what we are asking for happens. You are a daughter of the King, and you have been given access to talk with your Creator. Take full advantage of this freedom you have and abide in him. Idle thinking causes us to settle for what we desire right now. Abiding unlocks the will of heaven and gives us the grace to wait for what we desire most.

Abiding means we are considering the Lord in our daily plans, our responsibilities, and the commitments we say yes to. It means being still before the Lord and asking him what he thinks about our to-do list. When we seek him, he will show us what he is asking from us, where we should place our efforts, and how we should spend our time. Time with him reminds us that we aren't meant to do it all or to do it all perfectly; but in our weakness, we are made strong. He will reveal to you what to release and relinquish, and encourage you where you feel most defeated. As you respond to his leading, you will experience his grace. His grace that gives you the power to do all that's in your hands and wait with expectation for all that he has promised you. You will begin to walk in greater joy, knowing that what he has placed in your hands to do matters to him. No more striving for perfection, because you understand your strength comes from surrendering your everyday life to Jesus.

Take a deep breath in and exhale out; take the pressure off yourself! Do that a couple times if you need to, as often as you need to. And if you start leaning toward striving and feeling defeated, remember this: "But he said to me, 'My grace is sufficient for you, for my power is made perfect in weakness.' Therefore I will boast all the more gladly of my weaknesses, so that the power of Christ may rest upon me" (2 Cor. 12:9).

Resting

Honoring the Sabbath reminds us that it is not all up to us. Sometimes we think that to hurry the waiting process, we should do more. When we choose to rest in the midst of unfinished work or in the middle of what feels like a standstill in our waiting, we are relinquishing control and, once again, fixing our eyes on Jesus. It's a life-giving power move. The enemy of our lives wants us to stay busy and consumed. Rushed and exhausted, doing everything and anything, hoping that we can make it happen for ourselves. But when we avoid the trap of constantly moving and working and choose rest, the freedom we have in Jesus is on full display.

If you're anything like me, you might be rolling your eyes right about now. Girl, I get it.

I used to cringe at the word *rest*. When I would be at small group or meeting a friend for coffee, and someone would express how she was trying to rest more and explain to me the importance of honoring the Sabbath, I would about have a full-on panic attack. What I heard was "let's be lazy; let's be slackers." My response was always that there are people to reach, things to do, and a life to be lived, so why are we talking about rest? I came to realize they were talking about rest *because* there are people to reach, things to do, and a life that is meant to be lived to the fullest.

I have spent so much of my adult life doing my very best to bring honor to God in my doing, whether it's volunteering at my church, helping friends move into their new home, performing well at my job, or encouraging others through my writing. I love what I get to do, and I'm thankful that the Lord would give me the opportunity to be a part of his work on earth. And while I will continue to make it my life's mission to leave it all on the line and pour out my heart, my passion, and my resources, allowing God to write a great story with my life, I am learning more and more that in order to do that well, I must first learn to rest.

We can magnify the Lord in our stillness.

We are not God's workhorses, slaves, or hired help; we are his daughters! Just like the children of Israel needed to be freed from slavery, we also need to be freed from the mindset that God requires constant work from us. When we leave no margin for Sabbath rest, we express that it's all up to us! And even when it feels like that, it's not all up to us. We have a Heavenly Father who desires to display his goodness and faithfulness to us.

Our culture screams, "Hustle!" But our God says, "Be still, and know that I am God." This passage of Scripture, Psalm 46:10, is not written as a suggestion but as a command—a command to relinquish control, to let go, to stop from frantic activity.

Frantic activity.

The definition of *frantic* from Lexico is "wild or distraught with fear, anxiety, or other emotion." Friend, God's plan for your life does not include you being filled with fear and anxiety and moving with frantic activity. Society celebrates the exhausted woman; we give her trophies and applaud her efforts. She is known as a *Girl Boss*—whether her frantic activity looks like staying at home or building an empire, culture demands that she does more.

But frantic activity leads to an overwhelmed soul, no longer able to see God in the promise. God is not a dictator in heaven ruling over the earth. He isn't the universe unaware of your purpose. God is an intimate father, a God who cares for us personally. His desire is to know us and for us to know him. He doesn't dispatch purpose and promises so that we can go on ahead and complete the mission. Instead, when he shares a promise with us, he is extending an invitation to be a part of his redemptive plan for the earth. What does that mean? It means that God chooses us to be a part of showing the world just how much he loves them. He uses our story—the good, the bad, the suffering, the waiting, and the victory, all of it—to tell that story. This has never been a story about how awesome we are; it has always been a story about how great God is. In the midst of our messes, mistakes, and shortcomings, he still chooses us. He still chooses us to tell his story.

When we are still, when we pause, when we rest, when we turn the focus from our efforts and magnify God, we are reminded that God is capable, willing, all-powerful, and sovereign. When we are still, we put our priorities, fears, anxious thoughts, and dreams in their proper place. When we face trials and are tempted to get to work and fix whatever we are facing, we are comforted beyond measure if, instead, we choose to rest in a posture that says, "God, you are working in my stillness."

Sabbath rest has everything to do with how well we will run this race. Just like an athlete who puts her body to the test and understands that rest is a crucial component to her success, the same is true for us. No longer rejecting or cringing at the mention of the word *rest*, I have learned to embrace it more and more each day. Resting doesn't have to look the same each time, and it doesn't require you to visit somewhere tropical, though it is awesome when you can. Some days, rest has looked like me setting a timer for myself and sitting in silence. When my mind starts to wander or I start thinking about work, I redirect my thoughts and focus on being present. Some days, I delete apps from my phone and take a pause from work emails, status updates, or text messages.

Choosing to rest instead of work realigns our perspective. It debunks the idea that the early bird gets the worm and embraces a life-giving understanding that God is working in our work, in our rest, and in our waiting. He does when I refrain from doing, and he is the One who will bring it all into completion. He fills every void and does some of his best work in my stillness.

The good news is this—it's not all up to you! Rest in that understanding and walk in that freedom. Let's magnify the Lord together, not just in our doing, but in our resting.

Surrendering

We have all been there. Perhaps you are right there today—in a *funk*, experiencing emotions you can't quite articulate or explain. Nothing is terribly wrong, but everything isn't perfectly right either. Maybe you have found yourself saying:

> *I'm just in a funk.*
> *I just feel a little off.*
> *I'm so drained.*
> *I just can't seem to get motivated.*

However we express it, and whatever it feels like to us, it's commonly called burnout, and we can find ourselves there if we don't prepare for the middle properly. Whether you spend your weeks studying for exams, working full-time, volunteering at a non-profit, staying at home with your babies, or building a business, if you don't refuel, you are going to burn out.

Burnout is a result of running on fumes or pouring from an empty cup. As a result, the things that usually bring us *joy* are now becoming areas of *frustration* and *tension*. The *commitments* we have made now seem like daunting *tasks* that we desperately want out of. The things we have brushed over or the emotions we've allowed to lie dormant are coming to the surface. We are ready to quit, give up, or stop short.

On our journey from here to there will be unexpected hurdles and things beyond control. There will be moments that require us to show up even when we don't feel strong enough or equipped to carry out the task. Times when the hurdles on our path seem too tall or too scary and impossible to jump over. And sometimes, just as we gear up enough strength to clear the jump, we see another obstacle up ahead. And because we cannot afford to stop short or give up now, we must learn to prepare. We can't avoid the obstacles in our path, but we can avoid burnout. Here's how.

Armor Up

The first thing that pops up on my phone every morning is the weather forecast for the day. It lets me know how I should prepare as I get ready for my day. Looking at the temperature, I can decide if I'm wearing my coat, my scarf, or both. Just like I want to make sure I am prepared for the temperatures outside, I want to make sure I am prepared for whatever it is that I will encounter that day—whether at my job, at home with my family, or responding to text messages and emails. Spending time with God daily prepares me for what is ahead. It doesn't always look the same or go the same way every time, but it is nonnegotiable.

There are many mornings when I would much rather get right to my to-do list and work on things than read my Bible or pray. But the daily showing up reminds me that I can't do this without

God's leading. Spending time with God gives me perspective, grace, courage, and peace—everything I need to win the middle. Some days, I'm armoring up during a morning run, in my car, or in my room. No matter where, or the length of time, it is time set aside to hear from God.

Grow Up

When we aren't actively growing and putting ourselves in uncomfortable situations that promote growth, we will feel stuck. Everything about our nature is always adapting, growing, and reproducing. Being stagnant causes frustration. I make sure to find things that challenge me daily, weekly, monthly, and yearly. I have never met a person who was actively growing while experiencing burnout at the same time. Their lives were not void of hardship or resistance, but doing things outside of their comfort zone creates a resilience that is essential in their journey. We get more comfortable working our way *through* uncomfortable instead of giving up when it's hard.

Freshen Up

Find ways to breathe fresh life over your day-to-day. Don't let it become stale, but instead discover the new and beautiful in the midst of the ordinary.

Some days, I finish the day by writing down specific things that I am grateful for. Right now, I am really grateful for the new workout pants I was gifted for Christmas. Yesterday, I was grateful for the belly laughs I shared with my son at lunch.

When you know you have to write something down at the end of the day or week, you will not only look for the tiny moments that keep things exciting, but you will find them.

Check Up

Things get out of alignment and start to get off-balance. Although I never try to find the perfect balance for this adventure called life, I do try to find a rhythm. I create times to check in with myself and with my husband, to reevaluate where things are. We recognize what's not working well, what is demanding too much effort, and what is no longer yielding the return on our investment. It is a time to forecast what is on the horizon in order to make adjustments.

Refill yourself, stay committed to growth, see today with a fresh perspective, and check in with yourself often.

FIVE

Running *Behind*

God doesn't give us due dates, but he promises due season.

When a woman is pregnant, the doctors do their best to give her an estimated time of arrival for this bundle of joy. Now, having experienced three pregnancies and two births, I think it's baffling that doctors still give an expectant mother a due date. Of course, they preface this date with, "This is only an estimate and not a 100 percent certain date." But let's be real for a second—how many mothers do you know who didn't write down the exact date in their calendar as soon as they got home?

For the next several months, she will be asked, "When are you due?" People are excited that she is pregnant, and they want to know, "How long are you waiting?" Or, in other words, "When is that baby going to come out?" And, with all the confidence and eager smiles, she will repeat this date over and over again, to loved ones and to complete strangers in line at the coffee shop. Knowing when this baby is going to come out assures this mother-to-be that she will soon hold her baby in her hands. That is, until she clears the date when it's safe for the baby to come into the world, or until the baby is still cooking in that belly a few hours past his or her due date. What was once served as an assurance becomes a drudgery.

Those of you who have been pregnant and who have birthed a child are laughing right now, because you know it's true. It's all fun and cute until that baby wants to stay in that womb twelve minutes longer than you planned for. The exciting date on the calendar quickly turns into an eviction notice for the bun in the oven. You start googling all the ways to get that baby out of there, which include eating spicy foods while driving in a car on a bumpy road, to name a few.

The last few weeks and days leading up to that beautiful arrival seem brutal. Each passing minute seems endless, and there are even moments when you think, "Will this baby ever come out?"

Much like an expectant mother, we start to get antsy when we feel like we are past due on the thing we are wanting to see happen. Those anxious feelings turn into doubt, and the doubt weighs on us so much that we become weary. Perhaps that is where you are right now—weary as you wait on the promise. I have been there, and I still find myself there in moments when I forget that although God doesn't give me a due date, he has given me the promise that there is a due season. The same is true for you.

When I was pregnant with my son Jett, our twin girls were three years old, and we were weeks away from launching our church. I know—perfect timing. Because I had a C-section with the girls, my doctor informed me that we would need to have a C-section for him as well. So we put that date on the calendar and that was that. Until I decided I wanted to try to have him vaginally. So we switched our doctor and started planning for this guy to come all on his own, preferably the same day or before his scheduled C-section.

Jett had other plans. I surpassed that scheduled C-section due date by a long shot. Almost two weeks, to be exact. I was large, I was hot, and I was bothered. That due date fueled me with frustration, and every time I would walk into our room where we had his crib set up, it mocked me. *This baby is never going to come out. Doesn't this guy know we have a church to launch and things to do?* These were my thoughts for the days leading up to his much-awaited arrival.

I labored on and off for days. We would get some strong, consistent contractions and head to the hospital, only to be sent home because I wasn't ready. This went on and on. I was tired, I was weary. When I would look my doctors and nurses in the eyes with the most pitiful look, they would remind me that even though it seemed like eternity, I was going to meet my baby boy sooner than ever.

Days later, after twenty-four hours of active labor and countless hours of pushing, Jett still didn't want to come out. So, after all of that, I delivered my baby boy via C-section, ten days after his originally planned due date. When the doctor brought him over to me, I could have sworn Jett had a full beard like his dad and spoke in a deep voice, because the kid was massive. He weighed nine pounds and twelve ounces. The doctor laughingly joked about how this big guy should have been born weeks before. Who are you telling, Doc?

Our waiting can be grueling, and there are moments when it feels like it is never going to happen. Moments when what you have been believing for feels more like a pipe dream than a promise. But I am here to remind you that you are closer than ever. Even though it feels like an eternity, you are going to hold your promise—in due season. I don't know how it's going to look for you, and I don't know what the birth story will be when God brings forth all that he has promised you in your life. But I know that if God has promised you, he will make good on his promise.

We just can't give up. We must remain sure that even when it seems hopeless and even when we get tired, frustrated, or weary, God is in it and he will make it happen. "And let us not grow weary of doing good, for in due season we will reap, if we do not give up" (Gal. 6:9).

When I read this verse, I don't picture someone who has just begun, but I picture the athlete who is approaching the finish line. I picture the person who is so close to seeing that promise realized in her life. This girl has continued to be faithful year after year, month after month, week after week, and day after day. This girl is so close.

This is when we are the most vulnerable in our season of waiting. This is when we must guard our hearts and minds and remind ourselves of who God is and who we are in him. The enemy of our souls will try to convince us that it's never going to happen. As we see others experience what we are believing for, he will try and convince us that, somehow, we have missed the moment. When I was in the hospital, I remember hearing babies being born all around me. I would see women walking up and down the hall and then hear their family cheer with excitement as she finally brought that baby into the world. It served as encouragement to me, and, at the same time, it made me a little more anxious to have that moment too. Preferably right then and there.

Some of us have a laser-focused due date marked in our calendar that God has never given us. Some of us are weary because we are looking for a harvest that is not ready to be harvested. We are anxious and upset because we feel like our dreams and plans and promises are past due. When I first told others about Jett's birth story, I would speak about how late he came into the world. But when I did the math, I realized that Jett came right on time. Yes, it was two weeks after our originally planned due date. But the day he arrived was only two days after his actual due date.

Do you find yourself talking about your dreams as though they are late? Erase that due date you have etched on your heart and mind. If you have it written with lipstick on your bathroom mirror, wipe it off. If you have it typed up in an Excel spreadsheet, delete the file. If you have it color-coded in your five-year planner, toss it out. Believe today that God is always on time, even when it's not happening in your preferred time frame.

What Time Is It?

Weariness and doubt will rule our emotions if we are unable to define the season we are in.

"For everything there is a season, and a time for every matter under heaven" (Eccles. 3:1). We always want it to be harvest time, don't we? Harvest time sounds like a party, and I want to be at that party. But it's not always time to harvest. I would even take it further and say that most of the time it is *not* harvest time. There are a lot of days to sow, plow, till soil, water, and nurture the ground before ever seeing a harvest. Oftentimes, we view this waiting season as a day-after-day experience of walking outside to see if it's time to harvest, each time being greeted with bare land and no crops.

I was born in Silicon Valley, the land of iPhones and Facebook, so it's safe to say that I don't know a whole lot about farming. However, farming is mentioned quite often in the Bible, drawing parallels to our lives and giving us examples of how we ought to mirror our lives to that of a hardworking farmer. "It is the hard-working farmer who ought to have the first share of the crops" (2 Tim. 2:6). Notice it didn't say the *waiting* farmer, but the *hardworking* farmer.

We are not going back to that mentality that we have all the power to make the dream happen in our lives. We already silenced the lie that says it's all up to us. But we must realize that our time of waiting is not idle or wasted time. Our waiting season has purpose, possesses meaning, and has everything to do with harvest season. Without the hard work and the day-to-day obedience to show up and be faithful with the land God has entrusted us with, there is no harvest time.

Overnight Success

As we look over at the lives of others, whether we know them personally or not, it is easy to desire their harvest season. We say things like, "She is an overnight success!" "Wow! That was all of a sudden!"

But overnight is only what we see and the lie we believe. Our culture sells this to us with ads that promise a six-pack of abs in ten days or how to lose twenty pounds in three minutes—and we buy it every single time. We know that good things take time, yet we think that if there is something that gets me there faster, I at least want to know about it. If we had a conversation with a farmer, he or she would confirm that there is a lot of everyday, messy, hard work that happens before a single crop is ever harvested. And our season of waiting is ordinary and messy and requires us to keep showing up.

You know what pains me to even type, but I can't gloss over? The reality that even when we do the hard work, even when we show up, and even when we do all that has been asked of us, we still cannot control the outcome. A farmer also knows that there is a lot of risk involved and in spite of his hard work, the harvest is up to the Lord. We cannot control the storms of life, and we don't have the power to schedule them for a better time to come. There will be seasons when storms come blowing through our lives, and it will seem as though all our hard work, time, and effort was for nothing.

Our faith will be tested, our hope will seem dim, and our trust in Jesus may waver. If our focus is on the harvest, we will be disappointed. If we approach our waiting season as a time to get what we want, we will be disheartened. But when our focus remains on Jesus, and when our hearts remain surrendered to the One who is Lord of the harvest, we can remain confident no matter what it looks like.

Is that easy? No. The things we are believing for, the promises we are waiting on, and the dreams we are working hard to see happen are close to us; they are personal. It is painful when things don't turn out the way you imagined they would. It is gut-wrenching when what you are believing for hasn't happened yet. And it is grueling when all of your hard work doesn't seem to make a difference.

In the world, that would be the end of the story. But in God's economy, that is not the end. And even when those things happen or do not happen or haven't happened yet, he promises to turn all things around for our good.

Bless Her Heart

I was born and raised in California, but we have put down our roots here in North Carolina. People in the South are known for their sweet tea, southern charm, and one-liners delivered in the cutest southern twang.

"Bless her heart!" is a popular saying around the South that is often used when someone is going through a tough time and people feel bad for her. It can also be used when someone thinks a not-so-kind thought about someone else, but doesn't actually want to say what she is thinking. I have heard this saying more times than I can count, whether someone has lost her job, has a bad headache, is going through a divorce, or is struggling financially. No matter what it is, if what you are going through isn't desirable, you can count on someone using this statement to you or in reference about you.

When you and I are navigating our season of waiting, we will be faced with situations and circumstances that are not desirable. Our trials will seem to be taking us in the exact opposite direction of our promise and desired destination. We will be quick to blame the devil, our boss, or whoever we deem responsible for the storm. Some of us will send out a fleet of text messages to friends and family members begging for prayer. Our friends will agree with us and begin praying for our situation to go away and for whatever trial we are navigating to change quickly.

But what if the very things you are asking God to deliver you from are the very things that he has brought you to? God is a good God who does not dump his blessings on us but entrusts us with a promise and a story to tell about his goodness. Some of us are looking at the lives of others, and we feel bad for them and pity their lives, when in actuality God has positioned them right where he wants them. I am not saying that God does any harm to us, because he is good. But God does allow us to walk through storms and experience hard situations. Not without a purpose.

If God's sole purpose were to make us happy, he would give us what we want, when we want it, how we want it. But God is a good Father who gives us what we need, in his timing, in his way. He cares far more about who we are becoming than about what we are getting. Who we are becoming is developed in the waiting. That is why our waiting is necessary. This is our hope—if God's best work in us happens in the middle, we can rest assured that there is purpose in our waiting and that nothing is in vain.

I think about Jesus in the garden when he asks his father to remove the assignment of the cross from him. That if there was another way, he'd rather not endure what he was getting ready to walk through. Scripture describes this prayer as a moment of deep anguish. Jesus asked for a different outcome not once, not twice, but three times. Jesus in his sorrow cried out to God. Each time, he petitioned for God to intervene and to find another way. And then he followed his final soul cry with eight hell-defeating words—*not my will, but your will be done.* Jesus asked God the Father to deliver him from the cross, but God did not. And although Jesus's prayer did not change his situation, it changed him.

Some of us are asking God do deliver us from the very thing he has assigned us to. Some of our friends are praying prayers to get us out of the situations we are facing, when God is giving us an opportunity to get something out of what we are walking through. Some of us will not experience the miracle or the promise we are waiting for on this side of eternity. How could that be? If God is good, how come he doesn't heal every person who is sick and believing for a miracle? How can a good God allow bad things to happen to good people? Why would he choose to not change a situation when he has the power to?

If there were anyone who knew the power and the authority God the Father possessed, it was Jesus. Jesus in his humanity pleaded with the Father to spare him from the brutal death he was getting ready to endure. It's okay to want a different outcome, to want the story to be different, to want God to move quickly. But if we choose to submit our requests to him, we must also surrender the outcome, even if that means him choosing not to give us what we are believing for.

Prayer changes everything. It is the private and intimate conversations that we exchange with the Father that give us renewed strength and hope.

Prayer changes our posture in our waiting. It is where we get the strength and the courage to declare our desire to see God's will for us on this earth unfold.

Prayer changes what we pray. Spending time with Jesus aligns our heart with his heart.

Prayer changes how we interpret our waiting. We no longer see what we are experiencing as a result of bad decisions or mistakes.

When things don't happen the way we plan them to, we make quick judgments, oftentimes questioning the nature of God. We approach God as our personal genie in a bottle who is there for the sole purpose of giving us our wishes. But God is not a genie in a bottle. He is the King of kings and the Lord of lords. He is omniscient, sovereign, and omnipotent. Goodness is his nature and sometimes, no matter how much we want something, he doesn't give us what we want.

Are things falling apart or are they falling into place? Are you taking steps backward, or are you like an arrow being pulled back and positioned in the tension of a bow, ready to be released? The difference is how you choose to see it. If you have placed your life in the hands of Jesus, then you can trust that although it might feel like you are being pulled back, you are actually being positioned to be launched forward. If you have surrendered your life to Jesus, you can stand confident that even when things appear to be falling apart, they are, in fact, falling into place.

SIX

Training *Ground*

As I was gearing up for another day of writing this manuscript, my husband yelled from another room, "Hey Babe, have you heard of the new app? It's called Accelerate Reader, and it gives you the highlighted version of a book, taking out all of the fluff." Um, did he just say that? Like, right now, as I am getting ready to spend hours pouring out my best? And did he call it *fluff*? He later regretted this conversation.

I came storming in the room, stomping and being a little dramatic, yet still composed as I tightly gripped my coffee mug, trying not to slosh my coffee everywhere. "I am about to spend a few hours of my morning writing—it's not called *fluff*, by the way. It's called hard work—it's called hard-earned words—it's called sacred insight and perspective that is meant to be read and experienced." I went on. "This is what's wrong with our culture today—they don't want to *actually* walk through the process.

They want to cut to the chase, avoid the *fluff,* and just hear the good stuff." Yes, I even air quoted the word *fluff* with my fingers.

We were both sort of laughing at the irony about the moment. The idea of this new app paralleled with the concept of this book. He continued, "It says this is for people who don't have time to read through an entire book." I of course interrupted once again with a good ole, "How about they not spend an hour watching the news and actually read an entire book!"

Can you tell I was a little fired up? Okay, I was a lot fired up.

These days, we can say we've read an entire book without actually having to read an entire book. We don't want the "fluff"; we want to get straight to it. When I first began my walk with Jesus, I remember my cousin giving an illustration about how it often feels when we trust our lives to Jesus. She described how there are times when he shows us our purpose, and then it's as if he turns us around and points us in the opposite direction and says, "Okay, now go that way." At the time, I had no clue what that meant. In fact, the analogy confused me. Why would God do that? Doesn't this new life with Jesus mean easier, more direct? Doesn't this life with Jesus look more like Accelerate Reader?

For a long time, I adopted this idea that a life with Jesus meant life should be easier for me. That somehow, I should experience less frustration, pain, and resistance. I think when the American Dream became bigger and more ideal than God's dream for us, we began to embrace this idea that as Christ-followers, we have access to Jesus who is here to make us happier and more comfortable.

Jesus didn't come to make our lives easier, and he surely hasn't promised that we are going to get what we want, when we want it, how we want it. Somewhere along our journey, we've exchanged our holy surrender for idle striving. Nowhere in Scripture do I read about people who lived a safe and predictable life. Instead,

I read story after story about men and women of God whose lives got more dangerous after following Jesus.

We want to cut out the middle.

But without the middle, we are vulnerable, ill-prepared, and underdeveloped for our assignment. The fluff is the everyday, ordinary moments that most find meaningless. It's the desert place we don't desire to include in our highlight reel, and it's the process none of us wants to live through. So we search for the path of least resistance with no success.

Process for Promotion

One of my favorite people in the Bible is David. His story parallels the picture my cousin spoke about. Most of us know David as a great king of Israel, a man after God's own heart, but his story doesn't start out that way. David was a young shepherd. He was the youngest of seven sons. God was looking for a new king and instructed Samuel to go to the house of Jesse, where he would choose and anoint a new king.

The anticipation was palpable. Here came a man, sent by God, to secretly anoint the next king of Israel. One by one, starting with the oldest, Jesse presented his sons. But as each of the six sons passed, Samuel didn't sense that they were the chosen king. I can almost picture a room left wondering. If none of the six sons who were presented were the chosen king, then who could it possibly be? Jesse brought all of his sons except David to the anointing party, which makes it clear no one even considered David.

To take it a step further, when Samuel inquired about a potential additional son, Jesse felt the need to include David's lowly position of shepherd—surely not fit for a king, right? But David was in fact the one Samuel came to anoint. Mic drop moment, for sure. He wasn't invited to the party, then he was invited, then after all his brothers who seemed more kingly were denied, he was anointed right before their eyes. If I were directing this epic moment, I would cue the dramatic music as David assumed his position as king. But that's not what happened. David didn't get fitted for his new wardrobe, and he wasn't escorted by his new security detail to his new house. Where did this new king go, you ask? Back to the field to tend his sheep.

Wait, what?

If I were David, I would be looking for the Accelerated King version of the story—the one rid of the fluff that now includes me going back to the field, tending sheep. But David did go back to the field. David had just experienced the most monumental moment in his life, and moments later, it was back to business as usual, almost as if nothing had ever happened. I wish I could know the thoughts and feelings and confusion that David wrestled with back in the field. I insert myself into the story and draw parallels to moments in my life when it seemed God gave me a promise, God showed me something, and then, all of a sudden, I'm sent packing in the complete opposite direction.

This is where many of us find ourselves—caught in the tension between what we know in our hearts and the reality of our lives. This is the fluff most of us wish to avoid. But just as the field was important to David's future role as king, so is the field we stand in today to the future God has for us. David's role as a shepherd would prove to be an invaluable training ground for kingship.

When my son was small, and a little too young to play T-ball, we signed him up for junior T-ball, which was more of a clinic teaching the fundamentals of baseball. It was a big deal for us and we really got into it. For about six weeks, we spent our Saturday mornings on the field. Our twin daughters were into it the first two weeks, until they realized every week was the same, predictable drills. There were no hot dogs to enjoy, no one was keeping score, and no action was happening on the field. One Saturday morning in particular, one of our daughters asked, "When is Jett going to *actually* play baseball?"

I'm almost certain David asked God when he was *actually* going to be a king and do what kings do.

When Jett was learning to ground a ball, he was actually playing baseball. When Jett was learning to run and touch his foot on an orange plastic object, he was actually playing baseball. When Jett was learning to hold a bat in his hands and make contact with a ball, he was actually playing baseball. When David was watching and looking out for animals that might threaten his sheep, he was actually doing what a king does. When David was learning to use a shepherd's sling with persistence, he was actually doing what a king does. Just like my son wasn't ready to play in the World Series, David wasn't ready to assume his position as king . . . yet.

Maybe you aren't herding sheep or learning the fundamentals of baseball, but what is the field that God has assigned to you? Maybe you have a business idea in your heart, but you find yourself changing diapers and watching cartoons at home with your babies Monday through Friday. Maybe you desire to be a mother, and you are surrounded by friends who seem to get pregnant just by looking at their husbands. Maybe you have a ministry you want to start or grow, and your team looks like the Bad News Bears. Nothing about David's time spent in the field screamed, "That's fun!" But God in his mercy and grace figuratively turns us around and points us in what seems like the opposite direction, knowing it's in the surrender, it's in the messiness, where we are made ready for what he has for us.

So many times, I have fought against the field I have found myself in, at times cursing the ground that was assigned to build and shape me. I have wished away the opportunities, seeing them as mere distractions to my desired destination. I have let the tools in my hand become old and rusty, not knowing that I was holding a sling that could one day take down a giant in my land. I have despised the sheep entrusted to my care because they didn't look like the people I wanted to lead.

But David's time back in the field was invaluable. They were meaningful moments in developing who David was called to be. The lion and the bear he learned to wrestle would give him the courage to take on a giant in his land. The shepherd's sling he mastered would one day help him take down Goliath, a giant who intimidated all six of his brothers who were present that day long ago when he was anointed king. His look-like-a-king brothers didn't know life in the field. I am sure there had to be days when David resented his assignment to the field. I wish I knew what his brothers spent their days doing. I am sure whatever it was seemed more desirable than being where David was.

Just as David was left out of the moment to be anointed king, he was left out of confronting Goliath too. When his dad sent him to the battlefield, it was not with orders to save the day but with grilled cheese for his much more capable brothers. And here again we see David being obedient. If there were ever an opportunity for David to pull his "I am the king" card, now was the time to do it. But we don't find him doing any such thing. We find him with a bagged lunch in his hands serving his brothers. Surely there were better tasks for the soon-to-be king to do. Really, God, an errand boy? This is what you found fitting for David to do? The people of Israel are being tormented by this Philistine giant, and you want him to take the other men some food?

Imagine the moment David would have missed had he allowed pride to get in the way.

Opportunity usually hides itself in inconvenience. Whether it's the event we are bitter about volunteering for, the job we are dreading to go to, or the coffee meeting with a friend that we wish we could avoid, each of them have meaning and value. What seems like a huge inconvenience oftentimes is the sweet and divine setup from our Heavenly Father.

SEVEN

Fix Your *Thoughts*

It was the dreamiest December evening. Snow was on the ground, and the kids and I were headed to a fun outing. We were belting out Christmas jams, I was sipping my holiday Starbucks drink, and the kids were behaving. Thinking back, I can't actually confirm they were behaving because my music was turned all the way up, drowning out anything but "Feliz Navidad." All was merry and all was bright—until one single thought crossed my mind.

You're going to be embarrassed.

I went from experiencing joy to feeling so discouraged. It happened in seconds. I recognized what was transpiring, but I didn't try to fight back. Instead I let it continue. For a split second or two, I actually believed it. I believed that I was going to be embarrassed, that I was going to come up short and that my life wouldn't be significant. I've never desired significance in terms of fame or prosperity, but I want my life to be meaningful to God and to my family. My heart's desire is to leverage everything I have been entrusted with, living my life to its fullest potential. So maybe I should do more or try harder.

As a person who is always looking for ways to be better, personally, relationally, vocationally, it's easy for me to consider this thought process as a moment of personal development. Until I realize that these thoughts aren't leading me toward growth but are causing me to shrink back. I don't hear God audibly, but I do hear him in the thoughts that I think. And if these thoughts aren't rooted in love, building me up, encouraging me, or nudging me toward progress and greater surrender, then I know they aren't from him.

I'm pretty sure I had written the words "God, I trust you!" in bold at the top of my journal entry that morning. And I am almost positive I had posted a picture of me sipping coffee with an encouraging caption about how God can be trusted and how faithful he is just the day before. As a matter of fact, I think I wrote an entire chapter about the very thing that day.

Yet here I was.

Yes, I had written words of faith, encouraged others, and grown in my understanding of my thoughts and the power they have to steer my life. Taking control of our thoughts isn't a one-time miracle where we only think good thoughts forever after. Taking control of our thoughts is a daily, moment-to-moment decision. The enemy of our souls is persistent, and he doesn't let up. He is sneaky and will pester us any chance he can get.

So if these thoughts weren't coming from the Father's heart, they weren't the truth. In fact, I would go even further to say the opposite of those lies is the real truth. Our thoughts don't remain idle. They form roots in our hearts, take shape in our words, and become alive in our actions. The fruit is destructive. So was I going to sulk in this moment and allow these thoughts to rob me of my moment? Or was I going to choose differently?

Yes, we might not have any control over our situations but, friend, we do have control over our response. Our thoughts determine our words and our words shape our actions. We are what we think! Our thoughts are powerful, and although others don't audibly hear them, our thoughts are seen, heard, and felt in the way we live our lives, see the world, and interact with those around us. What kinds of thoughts fill your mind every day? Are they thoughts of worry, doubt, and insecurity? Are they thoughts of anger, sadness, and bitterness? The good news: no matter what we think today or have been thinking about ourselves and about our situation, we can change our thoughts!

We don't have to believe the lies; we can choose differently. Honoring God in the middle isn't just waiting it out, it's fighting our way through. It's choosing to rise above the temptation to think anything different about our situation or about our God.

As we pulled into the parking lot, I began to walk through my go-to thought battle plan. Here's what it looks like:

- **Acknowledge the feeling.** You don't earn a badge of honor for suppressing your feelings, and ignoring your feelings doesn't make them go away.
- **Identify the root.** Get to the bottom of it. What is making you feel this way? Where is this coming from? The thoughts that plague your mind have no authority over you. In fact, Scripture reveals to us that we have the power to arrest them. That we have control over them. "For though we walk in the flesh, we are not waging war according to the flesh. For the weapons of our warfare

are not of the flesh but have divine power to destroy strongholds. We destroy arguments and every lofty opinion raised against the knowledge of God, and take every thought captive to obey Christ" (2 Cor. 10:3–5).

- **Ask yourself what God has to say about it.** Search the Bible for his truth! When your heart is not anxious and your mind is clear, what do you really believe? Open your Bible and see what he has to say about it.

- **Replace your feeling with God's truth.** I cross out the lie and I replace it with the truth. "And now, dear brothers and sisters, one final thing. Fix your thoughts on what is true, and honorable, and right, and pure, and lovely, and admirable. Think about things that are excellent and worthy of praise" (Phil. 4:8 NLT). When thoughts of doubt, destruction, or insecurity cloud our minds, we must arrest them and then fill our minds with the right kind of thoughts. When we do, the God of peace comes to us.

- **Celebrate that truth.** I'm talking an all-out celebration! The kind of party where you put on your party hat, throw confetti in the air, turn the music all the way up, and shout from the top of your lungs.

When I do this, my posture, my position, and my perspective shift in a matter of seconds. I realize that it wasn't a lack of faith that was keeping me from seeing the truth, but it was my faith in the wrong things that was clouding my understanding of the truth. Not only am I no longer believing a lie, but I am now excited and expectant about something that was bringing me sadness.

No longer believing the lie that I was going to be embarrassed, I started to celebrate the truth that everything God has promised will happen. Nothing about my situation had changed. Yet, everything had changed. This is what joy looks like. Joy is rooted in truth while happiness is inspired by momentary situations. Happiness is fleeting; joy is constant and shows up even when proof of change is not yet visible.

Hopeful Anticipation

There was a particular school that we wanted our kids to attend. It is a great school with many families vying for a spot. We had applied two years in a row, and both times we were put on the waitlist. One year, we got the phone call we had been waiting patiently for, except it wasn't exactly what we were hoping to hear. The admissions office informed us that one spot had opened for our girls. We had twenty-four hours to decide if we wanted to make the change and enroll one of our twin girls in a new school, midyear, with no guarantee that her sister would get in that school year or ever. As a family, we prayed about it and felt peace that we were supposed to walk through this door that had opened for us. We sat down with the girls and let them know all the possibilities and discussed who would be the one to make the midyear move if we were to move forward.

We decided that Brooklyn was going to start at the new school. We all had a sense of excitement and apprehension, not really knowing how this was going to go. We had a few weeks before the official school year cut off during which Kennedi could get her call and join her sister. The girls especially were on an official countdown, knowing we were one day closer to the possibility of Kennedi not getting a spot. Finally, I got the call, but it wasn't the news we were wanting to hear. The deadline had come and no additional seats opened, which meant that we would have to reapply for the next school year, be placed on the waitlist, and pray that she would get her chance. Kennedi was well aware of the day, and the first thing she asked as I picked her up was, "Mom, so was this my last day at this school?" Man, it broke my momma heart to have to tell her that no, she didn't, in fact, get in the new school.

Kennedi burst into tears and declared, "But Mom, we prayed really hard and God knew this is what we really wanted!"

As I was pulling out of the parking lot, I said, "Okay, Lord, I guess this is the time to have this conversation, with a second grader who desperately wants to be with her sister at their new school." It was a hard conversation to have with my daughter. Everything in me wanted to give her good news that day. Yet, at the same time, I knew how important it was for her to learn the hard truth that God doesn't always answer our prayers how and when we want him to. Most often, our prayers are ushered in through situations, circumstances, and time frames we often try to avoid altogether.

We believed that God had opened a door for us to take our first steps toward having all three of our kids at this particular school. It would have been really awesome if both spots had opened for our girls at the beginning of their school year. Since that didn't happen, the next most awesome scenario would have been if the second spot had opened up. Since that didn't happen, we had some choices to make and decided to go back to the drawing board. Did we believe that God had led us to this point? The answer was a confident yes. So, if that was true, then we just as confidently had to trust that he was working out all the details, even in the waiting. My conversation with Kennedi went a little like this.

Did God hear our prayers? Yes.

Did God know that this was important to us and that we believed it would be a great thing for our family? Yes.

Do we believe he opened the door when one spot opened up for Brooklyn? Yes.

Do we believe that he can and will open the door for Kennedi and Jett? Yes.

Was it in our timing? No.

Was it our way? No.

So if all of that was true and yet here we are in the waiting, then we have to believe there is a reason.

I explained to Kennedi the hard truth that sometimes it doesn't happen the way we want it to happen in the time frame we are hoping it will happen. But if we have placed our trust in Jesus and believe that he can, even when he doesn't or when he hasn't yet, we must choose to trust him again and again.

If God is for me and if God is in this, then even this delay can be purposeful. Rather than wishing for a better outcome, Kennedi and I began to ask God to show us the purpose in this delay. We prayed and encouraged Kennedi and Brooklyn to seek God about this matter, to bring their honest disappointments to him and to ask him to show them his sovereign hand in all of it.

Can I tell you how incredible it was to see my girls open their eyes and their hearts as they searched for the purpose in their waiting? Two days after this hard, yet beautiful conversation with my girls, Kennedi jumped in the car and said, "Mom, I know the purpose. Marlee is my purpose. She doesn't know God, but I am someone in her life who knows God and who can tell her about him."

I don't know if Marlee is the only reason God allowed my girl Kennedi to experience waiting and the rest of her school year apart from her sister, but I know that Marlee knows about Jesus because Kennedi chose to see the God in the midst of her disappointing moment. We decided right away that we weren't going to give room for disappointment to grow or discouragement to cloud our hearts. Rather than dwell on what hadn't happened yet, we celebrated what God had already done!

Navigating two school schedules, pickups, and drop-offs was no easy task, but we knew that this season meant we were one step closer to what we were believing for. When we live in such a way, we will see the purpose in all of it, even in the most inconvenient, messy, and hard times. The same God who opened one spot for Brooklyn was the same God who could open two more for Kennedi and Jett.

Hopeful anticipation is not wishful thinking. Wishful thinking is superficial. Hopeful anticipation is supernatural—it takes inventory of what has been and what is and breathes faith over what has yet to be.

I love taking personality tests. For fun, when BJ and I were newlyweds, we would go to the local bookstore and spend hours learning what color, animal, number, and Disney character we were. On the StrengthsFinder in particular, positivity is one of our top two strengths. Positivity can come across as naive to most people. For some, the Christian faith seems more like a crutch or a thing for people living in denial or who lack depth. Put two positive people together, and you might think our life looks like a day at the happiest place on earth.

Embracing hopeful anticipation doesn't mean everything is peachy or that you are in denial. It's not looking outside and seeing a torrential downpour and saying the sun is out. It is saying that no matter what is happening right now, God is working in my waiting, God is moving on my behalf, and all things will work out for my good. It is looking outside and seeing the storm, but resolving that the storm will pass, remaining hopeful whether it takes minutes, days, or weeks to pass.

Did you know it takes an elephant nearly two years to birth a baby elephant? Let's break that down—twenty-two months! Amazed at this finding, I learned they have the longest gestation period of all mammals and are the largest and biggest-brained land animals alive in the world. Since they are not born at their adult size, it's safe to assume the development that happens inside the mother's womb is critical and necessary.

I already ruined your idea that pregnancy is nine months and told you it's more like ten months. I gave birth to my twin girls six and a half weeks early. Based on their birthdate alone, they had to spend a few days in the NICU. I'm so grateful they didn't have any complications and were only considered feed and grow babies. This meant they needed to learn how to work for food and grow, things meant to be learned and developed inside the womb. The gestational process is critical and important. And while there are great doctors and people who take incredible care of babies born too soon, everything a baby needs to grow and be fully developed is provided inside the mother's womb. The same can be true for us! We can patiently endure the season of our waiting with hopeful anticipation, knowing that we have been given the opportunity to grow.

Peace over Panic

It has been several months since I wrote the beginning of this chapter, sharing the story of one of my girls getting accepted into the new school, while the other didn't get a spot. Now, months later, as I make edits and add the finishing touches to this manuscript that you are holding in your hands today, we are still waiting for the phone call. All of our family and close friends are aware of our situation and are rooting for her to join her sister and brother (who got in as well) next year. This past week when I was talking with one of my friends, she asked me, "Aren't you worried about it?" With all assurance and peace, I said, "No, not one bit."

I have zero control of this situation and no amount of worrying is going to change the outcome. Rather than exhausting my time, thoughts, and emotions wondering *what if she doesn't get in*, we have decided to get really excited about the possibility of *what if she does*! We are in a holding pattern awaiting our clearance to land with a choice to make. Are we going to circle this situation filled with panic or peace?

The answer seems simple, right? But it's not always our most natural response. Sometimes being anxious or worrying about something gives us a sense of control—it's our way of keeping a grip on it. If we are weighing out all the options and pursuing all of the *what if?* scenarios, we think maybe we can find a way out of this thing. Choosing peace seems too passive. Shouldn't I be knocking on the doors of the school, demanding that they make an exception for my kid? But choosing peace isn't passive at all; in fact, it is a courageous position to take. Choosing to wait in peace is a declaration that says, "I don't know what the outcome will be, but I am confident that God is working things out for me."

We were crushing the new routine of taking the girls to their different schools, balancing their individual school schedules and commitments, only forgetting to pick up one kid one day. It was the only week I didn't check the weekly newsletter that informs us of special and early release days. One day while at work, I received a text message from my mother-in-law, letting me know that the school had attempted to reach me and my husband and that Brooklyn had been waiting for us to get her for over an hour. She offered to get Brooklyn and take her home until I could pick her up.

To make matters worse, it was Mother's Day weekend. So, I didn't feel like mother-of-the-year that day. All I pictured was my poor baby girl sitting on the curb, all alone, waiting for her mom. That last hour of work couldn't have gone any slower than it did. I left in a hurry and drove as safely and as quickly as I could to get my girl. When I picked her up from my mother-in-law's house, Brooklyn was smiling from ear to ear and greeted me with a hug. I spent a few minutes thanking my mother-in-law for picking her up and for not judging me in that moment.

I knew what I had to do next. I needed to turn this situation around with a trip to the ice cream shop. As we drove to grab a cone, and as I began to apologize to my daughter for the fifteenth time, Brooklyn settled me down with her words. "Mom, it is totally fine. You're fine, I wasn't worried one bit; I knew you'd come." When I asked if she was worried or felt alone, she reassured me that not only was she completely fine, but she was helping the office staff stack papers. Even with her reassurance, I still felt like ice cream was a good idea, probably more for me than for her.

Brooklyn had never been left anywhere before; and even though this was a new experience for her, she waited in peace, knowing that her mom would come for her. She never doubted or worried about it, because she trusts me, she knows that she is important, and she knows that we will always come for her. Over the past eight years, her dad and I have established trust with her, showing up for her since she was minutes old. When she would cry, we would tend to her needs; when she has needed us, we have always responded, nurturing her and communicating that in our care she is safe, valued, and never alone.

As children of God, we can experience peace in the middle of what seems like a holding pattern. Anxiety and worry are not par for the course only because that is how we have always responded.

We can choose peace because, over the course of our lives, God has established trust with us. He has showed up for us time and time again. In his care, we know that we are safe, we are valued, and we are never alone. We have access to a peace that surpasses all understanding. No matter how chaotic and uncertain we might feel, we can experience it. Choosing peace isn't turning a blind eye or avoiding our current reality, but it is choosing to remain sure that God's got this. As Paul comforted us, "Do not be anxious about anything, but in everything by prayer and supplication with thanksgiving let your requests be made known to God" (Phil. 4:6).

I am better at taking my fears to friends than I am about taking my requests to God. My friends are awesome, and I am thankful for their wisdom, assurance, and support, but what you and I need is time spent in prayer. And not prayers that are filled with worries, but prayers that are saturated with thanksgiving! Did you know that research shows people who practice daily gratitude are happier? I love that science supports the Bible! God gave us a weapon in prayer; he gave us access to peace in the midst of our waiting. When we take our petitions to God, we can be sure that he hears us; and not only does he hear us, he responds. He gives us insight, helps us see things clearer, and gives us peace when we might panic.

When planes are in a holding pattern, they have a specific route that they fly over and over again. I am sure it feels monotonous at times, circling the same thing over and over again. But the pilot knows that this is a necessary route. The pilot is in constant communication with the aircraft controller, awaiting clearance to land the plane. There are different factors that keep planes in a holding pattern, each of them for a purpose and a reason important enough to endure with peace.

Sister, you don't have to choose panic because you have always responded that way. Maybe today, rather than taking your *what if this doesn't work out* to your friends, you could take your *what if this works out for my good* to God.

EIGHT

Keep *Going*

There are some things that just sound fun—success, achievement, victory, to name a few. What about patience or endurance? Yeah, not so much. Not only do they not sound fun, but I try to avoid these two topics altogether. I heard someone say to be cautious when praying for more patience, because it usually means you will have more opportunities to practice your patience. I don't think I have prayed for patience since.

I love Orangetheory Fitness! It is a group fitness program that has been my jam for a couple of years now. And, most recently, it is where I became a fitness coach. The workouts are always different, challenging, and guaranteed to give your body the best workout. As a member, you never know what the workout is going to entail. It's not until you arrive that your coach gives you the inside scoop and lets you know whether it's going to be a strength, power, or endurance workout. When the coaches inform the group that it will be a power or strength day, almost everyone is happy, fully charged, and ready to go. But when we utter the word *endurance*, it's as if the enthusiasm walks right out the door.

Why? Well, endurance doesn't sound as fun as power or strength. We know that we are going to be challenged to go the distance and push beyond our current capacity. These days usually mean longer efforts and higher rep counts when working with weights—it's all about building stamina. The Lexico definition of *endurance* is "the fact or power of enduring an unpleasant or difficult process or situation without giving way." It is synonymous with the word *stamina*, which is "the ability to sustain prolonged physical or mental effort."

This still might not shout "Sign me up!" right? But, friend, these are two things you and I need to learn to embrace. No matter who you are or where you are from, you will face unpleasant and difficult moments and processes in this life. No one is exempt and no one has the ability to navigate around them, so we must learn how to endure them.

I used to see difficult moments as obstacles I wanted to get out of; but more and more, I have welcomed them, knowing that these moments are when God shows up, reminding me of who he is and reminding me of how strong I am in him. The enemy of our lives wants us to give up! He wants us to throw in the towel and give up before the appointed time. Patient endurance is not what we want, but it's what we need. The writer of Hebrews tells us why: "Patient endurance is what you need now, so that you will continue to do God's will. Then you will receive all that he has promised" (Heb. 10:36 NLT).

Where are my girls who desire to do the will of God? I know that's you! That is why you picked up this book and it's why you've made it this far. When we embrace the difficult, the messy, the hard moments and seasons and processes to see what God has promised come to pass, guess what? We will actually see it; we will actually receive it.

But we can't stop short—we can't afford to turn away now—we must endure. Patient endurance is what we needed then, and it is what we need now. I want to be there to see the promise fulfilled, don't you?

Most of us are great at starting something new! There is excitement and enthusiasm when beginning a new project. But not many of us are great at finishing. Not because we lack desire, but because we haven't learned how to navigate the middle well. The middle is not nearly as exciting as the beginning.

Just think about how exciting the beginning of a school year was for you as a kid. The thrill of picking out your school supplies and the anticipation of finding out what friends were in your classes. But talk to any student, parent, or teacher on March twenty-first, and they are never as excited as they once were.

Or what about the tangible momentum a new year brings? Everyone is eating kale, doing jumping jacks, and on track to read twelve books that year. After about fourteen days, the excitement starts to wear off, and this new reality isn't as fun and exhilarating as it was. So most people go back to what is familiar and give up on their dreams, goals, and what they are believing for entirely. We plan for the beginning, and we can imagine how sweet life will be as we cross that figurative finish line, but we don't prepare for the middle. More often than not, we don't consider the costs, or anticipate the bumps, pit stops, or necessary delays along the way.

Perseverance

One morning, I received a text from a friend stating that she was having a hard time sticking to her new workout routine and was needing some tips on staying motivated. I chuckled. That's an honest question for sure, but the raw truth is that no one—I don't care who you are—stays motivated.

Motivation is an emotion, not a position, and it should never be the driving force in our decisions. Navigating seasons of waiting and enduring the middle are made possible through perseverance. We don't need another pep talk or to post another catchy quote on a sticky note on our mirror to conjure up enough motivation. We need to go and do what we need to do no matter how we feel or what it looks like. For some of us, that is a practical showing up—to the gym, to our jobs, to the library to write another page on that book. For others, it's a spiritual showing up. It is a persevering through the emotions of doubt, hurt, and disappointment, and showing up with a heart open to God.

Keep on asking, and you will receive what you ask for. Keep on seeking, and you will find. Keep on knocking, and the door will be opened to you. That sounds fun only if I have to ask, seek, and knock one time. It isn't so fun when I have to keep doing it over and over again. It's frustrating and downright disheartening, actually. This scripture isn't for the beginner, or for the finisher, but for the girl right in the middle.

In recent years, I have developed a passion for fitness. A year after my third child was born and a year into our church plant, I realized that for the past two years, I hadn't taken care of myself physically. I decided this was not going to be a thirty-day goal, but I was going to commit to myself for the rest of my life. That meant no cleanses, detoxes, or crazy training: just me, showing up day after day. No matter how I felt, I showed up. Some days I looked and felt strong; and there were days that it just wasn't pretty. But I have persevered, through schedule changes, motherhood, a social life, vocational goals, trials, and the Christmas season. I have been showing up ever since. In the process, I have moved from feeling like it was an obligation to something I truly enjoy.

Working out has become a part of my life, and it has become something much more valuable than losing weight and burning calories. It's the territory where I have gained mental toughness to persevere. The mind is always willing to quit before the body is determined to finish. The showing up builds that mental toughness and muscle to push past the barriers and resistance that always come.

After several years, I began to serve as a coach and now have the opportunity to help people dig deep and persevere too. During the one-hour class, I coach members on the treadmill, rower, and weight floor. Unless you're an avid runner, time on the treadmill doesn't sound fun initially. Some days our efforts are longer than others, so it is my responsibility to let those running on the treadmill know where they are in their effort. Because I have endured these next-level workouts myself, I have become a better coach, knowing when and how to communicate to them in such a way that I don't let the wind out of their sails but give them the ability to press through.

It is incredible what one small word does for their mentality and ability to finish. Rather than saying they are not yet halfway through a long, uncomfortable effort, I will let a few seconds pass until I can let them know they are more than halfway through. When they know they have less to go than what they have already endured, what once seemed impossible becomes possible. The same is true for our own efforts. Some of us feel like we are stagnant and stuck right in the middle, when we are actually moving forward. Many of us are more than halfway there and closer than ever before to our promise and our desired goal. We need to develop the mental toughness and perseverance to endure the remaining effort.

I wonder how different the story would have been had Hannah stopped one prayer short, if she had allowed the discouragement to keep her from going to God one more time. Or what about Joshua and the battle for Jericho? God promised to give them the Promised Land, but a giant wall stood in their way. What if they didn't march seven times? What if they stopped on round four or even round six? God made them a promise, but it included faithfulness and trust on their part. What if they allowed what hadn't happened yet to keep them from what God was about to do? The walls of Jericho could not be taken down by their strength or by their might, but only by God's power.

It's hard. Sticking it out and enduring the process is hard. So is quitting. Giving up isn't the easier route. Perhaps it feels like that initially, but when you decide to start over again, you quickly realize that quitting was much harder than sticking it out. Maybe that is where you are right now, deciding whether you're going to quit or persevere. Maybe you're tired, tired of showing up and not feeling like you're making any progress and ready to give up altogether.

I get it. I have been there. It's okay to want to quit. Just don't actually do it.

And for those who aren't giving up altogether, I'll take it a step further and encourage you to stop changing directions! Stick it out. Do what you are doing, right where you are.

Keep putting in the work. Keep showing up. There's a quote that says, "The last thing to grow on a fruit tree is the fruit." The process is long and it doesn't often look like we are making progress. When we allow frustration to rule our emotions, they will get the best of us and convince us to stop short.

Friend, I know the journey has been tough, and perhaps you feel like you've been stuck in the middle. Let me encourage you: you're closer than you think. Don't give up on God, don't give up on you, and don't give up on what he has promised you. Perseverance doesn't always look loud and full of courage; sometimes it's quiet and steady. No matter what it looks like, or how you feel, show up one more time. This could be the time that changes everything.

My grandma Lydia has been instrumental in my faith journey. Since I was little, she has spoken words of affirmation over my life and has reminded me that God has a calling for my life. I always learn from her, and sometimes when I am talking to her on the phone, I take notes so that I don't miss a single thing. During one particular conversation, she said, "Sarah, keep trusting God, keep serving his people, keep doing what he has asked you to do, and believe that one day everything is going to be different." I'm glad I wrote that down, because now I get to share those words with you. Keep serving, keep showing up, keep believing, and keep going to God again and again, because one day everything is going to be different. One day, what is in your heart will be your reality. One day, what you've been praying through will become your victory story. One day, what was once not possible, will become possible. You're closer than ever, so don't you dare give up now.

The View Is Breathtaking

Just a few short hours away from our house is one of our favorite cities: Asheville, North Carolina. This cute city speaks all of my love languages, which include good food, good coffee, and absolutely breathtaking views.

That is exactly what we do anytime we visit, in that particular order. During one of our visits, we decided to take the kids along for the fun and went for a hike. The weather was perfect—the cool, crisp air had all the fall feels. The trail we journeyed on was just over a mile in distance, all uphill. One mile isn't too rigorous for me or BJ, but it sure is for our littles. And with only a couple of falls and a handful of stops along the way, we made it to the top. When we got there, you could hear the *oohs* and *ahhhs* from their little voices. One of them yelled, "We are above the clouds!" It was so exciting to see the wonder in their eyes. We soaked in the moment and captured the view. After a little while, we decided it was time to head back down.

As we were making our way down the mountain, we crossed paths with strangers who were hiking up the mountain. Each time we would say hello to someone new, our kids would shout, "The view is breathtaking, and it's worth it. Keep going!" Our kids experienced the beauty and the sense of accomplishment that comes only after a hard-fought climb, and they wanted to make sure others didn't miss out on that moment too.

Isn't that a lot like life, and doesn't it parallel the different seasons you and I experience? Some of us are enjoying the view at the top, others are making their way back down the other side of a mountain, and some of us are in the midst of a climb. On the journey, we can become tired, weary, and worn down and lose sight of our why. That is why we need each other! Our family had been to the top—we had experienced the breathtaking view, a view that is impossible to see in the middle of a climb. We need those who have gone before us and those who are experiencing a different season to share about their experiences with us. Not just about their mountaintop experience, but to share about the bumps along the way, their hard times, and the moments they wanted to quit.

Along this journey of navigating my waiting season and what has felt like an all-out climb, I have considered giving up and changing directions more times than I'd like to admit—but I haven't. Why? Because I have surrounded myself with other journeyers who reminded me about the incredible things on the other side of the hard moments and the long seasons of waiting. My friends have reminded me about the view from the top and have reminded me that this adventure, although it can be hard, is so worth it.

So here I am, in the middle of my climb, reminding you not to give up! Here I am encouraging you to stay with it, to keep putting one foot in front of the other, to keep your chin up, your chest tall, and your thoughts strong. While I've been on my climb, this scripture has given me life and I pray it does the same for you.

> Therefore, since we are surrounded by so great a cloud of witnesses, let us also lay aside every weight, and sin which clings so closely, and let us run with endurance the race that is set before us, looking to Jesus, the founder and perfecter of our faith, who for the joy that was set before him endured the cross, despising the shame, and is seated at the right hand of the throne of God. (Heb. 12:1–2)

Waiting seasons can empty us of our hope, and we can find ourselves flagging in our faith. The climb seems too steep, and it feels as though we are never going to get to the top. That is why we must fix our eyes on Jesus. He alone is our guide, and as long as our attention is on him, we can endure the season of life we are in.

· · · · · · · · ·～· · · · · · · ·

NINE

Nothing Is *Wasted*

*B*efore we got married, BJ and I shared our hearts and vision for our lives with each other. It was understood that we both felt called to pastor a life-giving church one day, and we were going to chase that dream down with all we had. Seven years later, that dream became a reality when we moved to South Florida and launched our church.

The year leading up to the big move across the country, BJ and I were writing out our goals, drafting up our plan, taking all the church planting courses, and doing everything we knew to do to prepare ourselves for the adventure of a lifetime. One morning I was praying and journaling, and I heard the Holy Spirit say this to me, over and over, until I finally accepted it and wrote it down: "Sarah, it's not going to happen the way you see it, but it's going to be everything you have ever hoped it would be."

Now, you can understand why I didn't want to hear this the first time. Before we ever began this journey, I had to understand that *this* dream, *this* vision, *this* beautiful story of God's redemptive love on display through a new church in South Florida was not mine to make happen, but it was for his glory and for his purpose. This statement bothered me and it frustrated me, but it became my saving grace in the season that awaited us. As we faced challenges, navigated tough waters, and went through what felt like hell, I knew that even though this was not how I would have chosen it to look, there was always a *but God* moment that interjected every single time, reminding me that it was not the end. This statement reassured me that my deepest desire and greatest hope for my life was very much a part of God's great plan.

Those words that were once whispered in my prayer time became louder and louder with every timid step of faith moving forward. I understood it now—what once sounded more like a God who laughs when you tell him your plans now sounded more like the God who makes all things work out for your good. I wish I would have let that statement really penetrate my heart the way it should have, because that moment in prayer marked the beginning of a wild adventure. I would soon face many more obstacles and hard moments that left me questioning God's goodness in my life.

As I write these words to you today, my prayer is that the truth about God and his actions toward you would penetrate your heart and that you would be fully convinced that God is not out to get you, trick you, or mock you. God loves you and is for you.

That's Not Fair

If you have been around church for a while, you may have heard the saying, "Favor ain't fair!" It's usually said when something awesome has happened to a person—a job promotion, finding cash on the floor, or maybe even a parking space up front. People use it to exclaim how God loves them so much that he gives them a little extra dose of love. Kind of like extra credit or a free side of guacamole. It's usually done in a casual manner, most often jokingly drawing the conclusion that God did this for them.

We see the word *favor* throughout the Bible. One particular time I want to highlight is the story of Mary, the soon-to-be mother of Jesus. Mary was *favored* by God. Out of all the girls, he chose her to be the one, to be the mother of Jesus. She was a virgin, about to be married, minding her own business, when out of nowhere things got a little weird. Okay, a lot weird. She was greeted by an angel and was given the information that she would become supernaturally pregnant. In case you were wondering, this wasn't a normal thing, not then and surely it wouldn't be today.

It was bizarre, yet holy. What an incredible, sobering moment for Mary. It was such a breathtaking moment; Mary was fearful, not truly understanding all that this angel who was sent by God was saying. Mary was going to have a son, God's son. He would be given the throne and would reign over the land forever. Sounds pretty epic, doesn't it?

As epic as that sounds, there were probably waves of doubt and uncertainty and questions swirling in Mary's mind and in her heart. How was she going to tell her soon-to-be husband? What was he going to think? And her friends, her family? What would they say? What about the life she had planned out, the dreams in her heart? Did this mean those were no longer for her to chase after? I would love to know what plans Mary had penned in her journal, what dreams she had deep within her heart, and what prayers she had prayed leading up to this moment.

I feel like all of those things played an important factor in God choosing her. What we know of Mary is that she wasn't from a wealthy family, she wasn't part of a well-known family. If she were on earth today, I doubt the world's view of who is successful or *favored* would think much of Mary. It's important we pause here for a minute. Every part of this story has meaning and value, especially this moment, when the girl next door is chosen to carry the King of kings and Lord of lords. So often, we see others living out and experiencing something we desire to have or experience, and we fall into the trap of thinking it has something to do with anything other than God's work in their lives.

Considering her reputation that was on the line, the relationships that could be potentially lost, and her life that would never be the same again, Mary declares who she is: God's servant.

This response says, "God, have your way in my life. No matter the cost, no matter the sacrifice, I am willing to be used by you. Not my will, but your will be done."

Favor comes with a high price; favor means laying down your life and surrendering your will to the Father, no matter what it looks like to you or to others. Mary's promise was that she would be the mother of Jesus—a king! That sounds amazing—that's when most would say, "Sign me up!" But when you see the figurative job description, that's also when most of us would opt to sit this one out.

"Let it be according to your word."

As Mary uttered those words, she was declaring her complete surrender. She would do this many more times in her journey ahead. Mary's life was marked by suffering. After her soon-to-be husband planned a way to leave her, he then decided he would get on board. And after she carried baby Jesus in her belly in the midst of haters, she and Joseph were forced to return to their hometown of Bethlehem. Mary's doctor should have put her on the no-fly list because that baby was on his way! But Mary didn't get that opportunity to nest—to put together the ideal nursery, to rest, to soak in the final moments before becoming a mother. No, instead *favor* led Mary to get on a camel and endure a long journey. Upon arrival and finding no other place to stay, Mary, who was now very pregnant and ready to deliver her promise, found herself in a stinky, dirty barn. I am certain this was never how she imagined it would be. I am certain this wasn't a part of her five-year plan, or something she desired her life to look like.

Favor doesn't usually look like favor. Knowing all that we know about Jesus and all that he would do for you and for me, it's still hard to draw a connection from Mary's first epic encounter with the angel to this moment right here. Mary understood something that many of us so desperately try to run away from. Serving Jesus and living out the promises he has made to us will cost us everything. Not because he is taking something away from us, but because he is including us in his redemptive plan to rescue all of humanity. His love for us is so big, so deep, and so wide that he will allow momentary heartache, seasons of waiting, and times of great adversity for eternal purposes. Does that make it easy? No. No, it doesn't. But it serves as grace for us in the middle of the most challenging, gut-wrenching, lonely seasons of our lives. It serves as hope that he has not forgotten about us, that he has never left us, and that he is with us always.

It's crazy how we can look at the life of Mary, at the lives of others in the Bible, and at the life of Jesus and somehow expect and even demand that we ought to get everything we want, how we want it, and when we want it. We are Christians: Doesn't that mean we should have this favor cloud that hovers over us when we are looking for a parking space, when we go for the job promotion, or so we can find five dollars on the ground?

No. When we choose to follow Jesus, when we utter the words "Let it be according to your will," we are saying we will trust God even when we can't see his hand. It means that even when he allows things to happen or not happen, we will choose to remain. We will choose to shout, "We are the servants you are looking for!"

When we first heard about this reckless, over-the-top love God has for us—that he sent Jesus to be born on this earth, to live a sinless life, to be executed for our sins, to pay a price we could never pay, and to be raised to life again, proving his love for us and sealing our place in eternity—we were so overwhelmed, so grateful, we responded with acceptance and surrender. Somewhere along the way, we exchanged that holy response to follow Jesus for comfort and convenience. Somewhere along the way, we started to sit comfortably in coffee shops to post catchy scripture verses on our social platforms and to have conversations with others who already know about this love, wondering and waiting, trying to discover our purpose and looking for ways to make life better here on earth.

This life is only the first step, and Jesus didn't come to make life more comfortable or easier for us. He came to make the impossible possible, to set the captives free. To give us life and life more abundantly!

Be That Girl!

A secondary, yet important, story unfolds here too. When the angel appeared to Mary, he disclosed that her relative Elizabeth was also pregnant. And when two preggers meet, something so special takes place. As Mary walked in through the door, and as the two ladies exchanged smiles and greetings, it made the precious promise in Elizabeth's womb leap, and she was overcome with great joy!

Isn't this the way friendship ought to look? If I were there that day, I feel like I would have initiated a group hug! Think about it for a moment—Elizabeth was barren, old in age, and she found herself finally carrying a child. The son she was carrying, John the Baptist, wouldn't be just any child. He would be someone filled with the power of the Holy Spirit. He would go ahead of Jesus, preparing the way.

Now Mary, with child, still unsure of all that was to come for her, was told by the angel that she was not alone in this journey. This moment was meaningful for both Mary and Elizabeth. The beautiful and breathtaking exchange between Mary and Elizabeth caused both of them to be filled with great joy as they realized how God was working in this mysterious and unusual way. And not only was the evidence of his hand becoming more certain, but the two of them shared in this experience together. What a gesture from heaven!

Mary's response was overwhelming as she recounted ancient Scripture from the Old Testament. From the abundance of her heart, her mouth spoke. She was beginning to see it more clearly, that this is what favor looks like, that this is what favor feels like. She was overcome with great joy, and from her soul she sang praises to God. In her waiting, in her unknowing, in her surrender, she was seeing the hand of God at work in her life and in her friend Elizabeth's life.

I wonder what those three months together looked like for these mothers-to-be. I can picture them watching their bellies grow while sharing stories of their encounters with the angels. Most certainly exchanging thoughts like, "Can you believe my husband was going to leave me over this?" And, "Can you believe my husband was a mute because he didn't believe the angel?" These two were soul sisters, and the gift of their bond quieted their anxious hearts, and both of them were filled with great joy.

As I look back over my life, God has gifted me friendships that I knew were orchestrated by his hand. There have been women in my life who championed me, women who helped me see God's hand at work in my life in the midst of hardship and trial. God will send you people too. It's possible he already has, and you don't see her as a soul sister for your journey, but as a competitor to your dream. Mary and Elizabeth needed each other during the beginnings of this new journey they were about to embark upon. And so do you—you need others to speak life into your journey, to remind you of God's promises. It's why I felt compelled to write this book. My prayer is that the words penned in this book bring you great joy, sifting through the noises of doubt, anxiety, bitterness, and hopelessness.

We need girlfriends who, when we leave time spent together, inspire in our hearts a song that is bursting out from our lips. We also need to be the kind of girlfriends who inspire others to go and do the same when they leave time with us. Let's be the kind of girls who will cheer for the girls on our left and on our right. Let's be the kind of girls who are committed to cheering on their sisters as they run their races, cross their finish lines, and dare to begin.

TEN

Start with the End in *Mind*

When I was growing up, my grandmother Sara always had a book in her hand. Her favorite has always been a romance novel with a good story line and life lessons learned along the way. When I was little, I saw her grab a new book from her "to be read" book pile and immediately go to the last chapter. I asked her if she was finishing the book or just beginning, and she said that she always reads the last chapter first. "But, Grandma, you're going to know how it all turns out! Why do you start with the end?"

"I read the end because I want to know that my time spent reading has a good ending, leaving me happy."

She gets just as involved with the characters and the story line, wanting them to end up happy or to experience the lessons they learn along the way just as she would without knowing the end. Knowing the final chapter reassures her that her time, her attention, and her engagement is worth it. She doesn't know *how* the characters will arrive at their final destination, how they will fall in love, or why only a few characters are mentioned at the end. But she does know that, in the end, it worked out, they fell in love, and perhaps they lived happily ever after.

Yet even in the knowing, there is still a story worth reading. We know how this ends; we know that God is the victor, and we know that as his children, we have the victory, but there is still a story worth living. Opening the pages of the book, we know that from where it begins to where it ends, there are unexpected turns, new characters, hardships, sweet moments, and exciting territory to cover. So much more than arriving to that destination safely, we witness firsthand how these characters matured, changed, learned, and grew into their ending chapter.

When we set out on this adventure called life, and when we find ourselves navigating time in the middle, we can experience the same confidence. Although we do not know how or when or even what we will experience along our journey, we do know the ending. Before we ever got started, God gave us his Word, the Bible. He gave us a glimpse at the final chapter before we even began. The final chapter reassures us that no matter what we face, no matter what we walk through, we win! We win because Jesus rose from the grave. We win because in our brokenness, grace came down and made us whole. We win because in our inability, Jesus gave us himself so that in all things we have victory.

Rather than approaching the chapters of our lives with fear or insecurity, fighting *for* victory, we can approach every obstacle, unknown outcome, tough moment, and unfamiliar territory *from* a place of victory. Victory is ours to possess right here and right now. When we experience setbacks, hardship, and heartache, we know that even if we don't know how we will get to the other side of it, we know that we will. When we approach a mountain of what seem like impossibilities, we can with confidence declare that God has already made this mountain possible to climb.

In every season, and with every step, let us start with the end in mind. There is always a story to tell! The ending makes the middle worth living through, but the middle is why the end is worth telling. Through a dream, an angel revealed to Joseph the final chapters of his story. Knowing the plan God had for Joseph gave him the strength he needed to persevere through the many highs and lows of his story. If we were only reading Joseph's final chapters, we could naively conclude that he was entitled or that he somehow lucked out to be ruler of Egypt. But when we start to get involved in his story, when we insert ourselves right in the middle of his story, the whole "he gets to be a ruler" thing doesn't look so glamorous after all.

At the age of seventeen, Joseph thought it was a good idea to tell his ten older brothers that one day he was going to rule over them. To make matters worse, his dad loved him more than he loved his brothers. He was the sibling that got a free pass when he did something wrong, he was never to blame for the fight that he clearly started, and I am sure he was given an extra gift or two at special times. Have you heard about the guy with the coat of many colors? That's Joseph. His brothers were already very aware of their dad's love for him, but to really make sure everyone knew, Jacob gave Joseph a coat of many colors. I'm sure you can already see where this story is headed.

For starters, this was probably not the smartest move. He shared about one dream where he was ruling over his family, and *then* he thought it was a good idea to share *another* one. But think back to your seventeen-year-old self, and you can understand Joseph's naivety expressed here a little better. Poor Joseph, *bless his heart.* His dream sounded pretty cool, right? He was going to be a ruler! It would be awesome if the next scene described how he became a ruler, and his dad and brothers were forced to get on board. But that's not what happened. What happened next was a series of from-bad-to-worse moments that Joseph lived through.

First, Joseph's brothers plotted to kill him. Before they could go through with their plan, his older brother decided killing him wasn't the best thing to do, so they decided to throw him in a well instead. After stripping him of the coveted coat of many colors, they threw him in a well. To ensure he wouldn't be found and that they wouldn't have to deal with him again, they decided to sell him into slavery.

While Joseph was enslaved to an Egyptian master, the master recognized God's hand on Joseph's life and made him his attendant. Then the master's wife begged Joseph to sleep with her, and when he resisted the temptation, she lied to her husband about his intentions toward her. So Joseph found himself in prison. While in prison, Joseph interpreted dreams for the pharaoh's cupbearer and baker, who were also in prison. He urged the cupbearer to remember him when he was freed. The cupbearer forgot about Joseph. Years later, Joseph was able to do a favor for the Pharaoh, and then he found himself second-in-command over all of Egypt.

It's easy to brush past the details, the time, the waiting, the pain, and the suffering that we find in Scripture. That's why I shared as much of this story as I did. If you have never read Joseph's story, I encourage you to. Some of the most incredible stories I know are from Scripture—Hollywood doesn't hold a candle to what we read about in the Bible. If this were a movie, we would see this story go from bad to worse, and with each change of scene, we would see these powerful words come up on the screen just as they do in the Scripture:

"And God was with Joseph."

Throughout his story, these five words are woven into every twist and turn that Joseph experienced. How could this be? How could a good God allow such horrible things to happen to Joseph? Being an outsider looking in, it does not look like God was with Joseph. If God was with Joseph, he would have prevented him from being thrown in the well, or sold into slavery, or wrongly accused. God could have helped Joseph avoid all the drama, all the hardship, all the pain, and all the waiting.

God of Miracles

When we first moved into our new home in North Carolina, we were in awe. Becoming first-time homeowners was a twelve-year dream that finally came to pass. Before move-in day, I remember walking through the empty home and envisioning this new life. We imagined the dinners we would eat around the kitchen table, started drawing up plans to paint, planned to add a few things here and there, and of course, made a wish list for our someday plans. We used the money we had saved up for the big move to do the small, important projects first, keeping our wish list for one day close by.

About a month later, the kids and I were coming home from school pick up to finish packing our bags and organizing our house before heading out for a weekend trip. As we walked up to the front door, one of my daughters started repeating, "Oh no, Mom, this is not good!" I of course assumed one of the dogs had gotten out and had made a mess. As I got closer to the door, I heard the sound of rushing water. It was so loud, it sounded as if we were standing close to a waterfall. Well, we in fact were standing next to a waterfall. Except this waterfall was in my house. Water was pouring down from my ceiling and coming out of every air vent and light fixture. I was suddenly standing in almost two inches of water, in my living room. Our new house was flooding. I got the kids out of the house and ran up the stairs to check to see where this water was coming from. A toilet upstairs had broken, and the water had been overflowing for the length of time it took me to pick the girls up from school.

The day before this ordeal, I had changed one of my fun letter boards from "Love Is Patient" to read "He's the God of Miracles." It was so sad to see our new home covered in water, and it was tempting to start panicking at all the work and effort it would take to get our home back in order. BJ rushed home to greet us, and the two of us stared at our house. We realized in this moment we had a decision to make. Were we going to panic? Or were we going to believe what we had so enthusiastically declared on our letter board? We decided to go with the latter. We looked at each other and said, "Okay, God. We are believing for a miracle."

It was a mess and it was a lot of work and effort for the next six months. Our house was turned upside down, and life felt very chaotic most days. There were moments I felt very weary and beat up. Our new home that was supposed to serve as a refuge and a place of rest in our new season in North Carolina was displaced. Only a small love seat survived, and let's just say it didn't quite fit the five of us plus the two fur pups. We spent a lot of time in our bedroom for family movie nights, trying our best to make the most of the crazy situation. When we would feel overwhelmed, we reminded ourselves that it was not always going to be this way and that God was the God of miracles.

Remember that secret wish list we had put together the day we moved in? Because of the amount of damage the water had done to our ceiling and our floors, forcing us to replace most of them, we were able to cross a few items off our list. It was a lot of work, and when it was finally all done, we were tired. But that interruption ushered in the miracles of God, providing the desires of our hearts. Would it have been nice to find a blank check written out to us for the purpose of remodeling our home? Yes. Would I have loved to get a call from Chip and Joanna Gaines informing me that we were chosen for a *Fixer Upper* episode? Yes, yes! But that's not what happened. I'm not saying God caused my house to flood, but I do know that he allowed it. And when our situations are left in his care, he promises that he will turn all things around for our good! We just have to be willing to look for him in the middle of it.

There are a lot of different ways I would write up a story for Joseph. I assure you, none of them would include any of the trials he experienced. Thankfully, I am not God. I don't know why God allows certain things to happen. I have some questions for him on the other side of eternity. But what I do know is that even in the pain, the suffering, and the hardship, God was with Joseph.

God was with Joseph. Over and over we see this declaration woven into his story. These four powerful words give me peace for my today and confidence for my tomorrow. I know that no matter what I walk through and experience, God is with me too.

When Joseph was reunited with his brothers, the Bible specifically mentions the moments he wept. It was evident that Joseph's pain was real and raw and that he had endured a lot since the last time he'd seen them. When he finally had the ability to speak to them, he did not ask questions or point fingers. He brought meaning to all that he had experienced. Yes, they might have sold him into slavery, but it was God who sent him. Although situations and people played a role in his story, God was with him, God had gone before him, and God was using these circumstances for a purpose.

Joseph had every right to be angry toward his brothers, to be bitter about his story, and to be suspicious of God. But just as it is written that God was with Joseph, Joseph's response proves that Joseph was with God too. Joseph still had a part to play in this story, in how he responded to God's presence. Friend, I am here to remind you that no matter what your season of waiting looks like and no matter how distant what God has promised you seems to be, God is with you and he means it for good. I have no doubt that God will make good on everything he has promised, but you too have a part to play. What's your part? To look for God's hand at work in your life, in every season. I believe that's what Joseph did. He looked to see God's work in a dark pit, as a slave, in a prison, and as a powerful ruler who had the power to take matters into his own hands and get even with his brothers.

His life was his assignment, and your life is yours. Your waiting is not your prison but your preparation.

God is a good Father who does not dump his blessings on us, but entrusts us with a story that reveals his glory and displays his work in our lives. We ask for healing, for strength, to be used by him and to experience the life he has for us. And it often comes by way of a process we resist. We then start praying for him to deliver us from the very thing he has brought us to. Sometimes, we even become offended by him, feeling as though he isn't listening to our cry.

Because Joseph was a real person, we can conclude that he experienced these moments too. Moments when he wanted to be delivered from the situation he found himself in. Remember when he told the cupbearer to remember him and tell Pharaoh to get him out of prison? It took more than two years for that to finally happen. Joseph wanted out! And maybe you find yourself there, wanting out of the season of waiting that you are in. But what if the very thing that you're resisting or praying will go away is the very thing he has brought you to so that you can be prepared for what you have asked him for?

We must trust the process, remain hopeful, and resist the temptation to doubt God's hand at work. He is with you and considers you so much that he will allow you to walk through the trials, the waiting, the mundane, the silence, the betrayal—all of it to bring forth the desires of your heart.

ELEVEN

Faithful to the *End*

Before the end of every year, I prayerfully consider what word God is speaking to me. This word serves as an anchor through the changes of seasons and experiences over the next 365 days. Some examples of my word of the year are *fearless*, *stand*, and *freedom*. Once I land on a word I believe God has led me to, I commit to the word all the way. I usually go all-out! I have the word written on something visible in my home, I shop for journals that have the word written on the front cover, and if I'm lucky, I'll even find a new coffee mug with my word of the year. This particular year was no different. Weeks before we rang in the new year, God gave me my word: *Inconvenient*. Wait, what? Yeah, my thoughts exactly. I was hoping for a word more to the tune of *adventure*, *harvest*, *blessing*, or *abundance*. Now that sounded a little more like the year I wanted to have. Inconvenient? That's not something I want to have printed on a T-shirt and post on Instagram, am I right?

I tried to dodge this word about seventeen times. Surely that was not *the* word. Maybe it was supposed to be a blog post or a message I would deliver for someone else? But just like the Krispy Kreme *Hot Now* sign, there was no avoiding it. So I caved and reluctantly declared it to be my word of the year. As I tried to imagine what this would mean for me and for my family, I did some inventory of the years past. When God gave me the word *fearless*, I experienced so many moments where I had to push past *fear*. When God gave me the word *stand*, I felt as though the waves of life kept crashing in on me and, wave after wave, I had to choose to stand. When God gave me the word *freedom*, I had to face the hidden areas where my trust wasn't rooted in Jesus in order to live in freedom.

Each word sounded more promising than *inconvenient* at first, but the process that I had to endure to see those words become fully developed in my life looked like trial, hardship, lack, insecurity, and change. The 365 days and opportunities to grow into those words didn't always give me the warm fuzzies.

Could God have made me fearless in an instant? Maybe so, but that is not how he works. When God gives us a glimpse of the forecast ahead, it doesn't usually look like what we see.

Mermaid Tales

Living in South Florida, we had perfect winters and sunny summers! And by sunny, I mean hot. In order to survive the entire summer, you needed to be at the beach or at the pool. So we made sure to introduce our girls to the pool when they were babies. No matter how intentional we were about exposing them to water, it seemed as though they wanted less and less water in their face every summer. One year, we decided to enroll them in swim lessons because their hesitation—okay, their extreme dislike for water splashing in their face—was a bit dramatic. Imagine bathing a cat, only much worse.

Leading up to their first official swim lesson, we made sure to talk it up with the girls. We wanted them excited. For the most part, they were eager to learn to swim like big girls. On our way to the first swim lesson, Brooklyn was sharing all about her excitement and expectations for the morning ahead. She is a lot like me, always way in the future and mapping out all the details. She described what the pool looked like, what her instructor might look like, and how many kids would be there, and she included a small detail that *Jesus was going to give her and her twin sister, Kennedi, mermaid tails so they can swim.* Nope, they weren't going to have to actually learn how to swim and put their heads under water; Jesus was going to give them mermaid tails.

This is the moment when after sharing this adorable story, we respond with, "Oh, kids, don't they say the darnedest things?"

Except for this time, maybe the saying "The apple doesn't fall far from the tree" would be more appropriate, because I have for sure believed God was going to supply me with a mermaid tail a time or two. Okay, perhaps I didn't say those exact words, but sometimes I feel like a spy or some sort of special agent trying to figure out how God is going to provide or answer my prayers. I can become pretty creative at times, coming up with grandiose ideas for how he will do something in my life—a lot like Jesus giving me a mermaid tail! When I ask for patience, I envision that he will give me the patience of Mother Teresa. Boom! Here is your patience, just how you asked for it, when you asked for it.

But it doesn't usually happen that way. Instead of zapping me with patience, he usually gives me opportunity to show patience.

Times when I desire to be more generous and I envision him giving me more resources so I can be generous, he shows me more opportunities to give from what I already have. It's not that God hasn't answered my prayers or that he hasn't honored my audacious prayers or creative imagination, but God sees the whole picture. He is our Heavenly Father who desires to give us good gifts!

How cool would it be if Jesus gave Brooklyn a mermaid tail so she could swim the ocean? Pretty cool, but it wouldn't be what she really needs or is capable of handling. There are lessons to be learned and healthy limitations and boundaries that need to be respected when a four-year-old is learning to swim. When you're learning to swim, you aren't just learning how to swim; you're also learning to trust, you're developing endurance, and you're gaining in strength—all things that are necessary to becoming an efficient swimmer.

I love Brooklyn's childlike faith that was displayed that day and her belief that Jesus could do anything. Because it's true: he can do anything. Nothing is impossible for him! He could have even given her a mermaid tail if he had chosen to. But even when he doesn't give us mermaid tails, he is still faithful. Brooklyn saw swimming as an easy thing for God to give her, instead of seeing it as something she would have to work hard for and develop and grow into.

Under Construction

Construction always takes longer than anticipated. My husband works in construction, and it doesn't matter how small or big, how standard or detailed the project is, it is always completed a day later than anticipated; in some cases, it's many days later. Unlike some contractors, he has learned the importance of never overpromising a completion date; instead, he plans for unexpected work. Yet even with his conservative estimation, building something always takes longer than desired. With these fixer-upper projects, the removal of the old comes first, in order to build something new. It is in this step that he and his crew find things hidden beneath the surface that often create more work.

During one summer, he and his business partners took on an outside deck project. When they went to do the initial cost and time estimate, they noticed that there were two old decks, built on top of one another, instead of the one deck they expected. The previous builders decided that, rather than tearing down the old deck, they would just cover it with new wood. What seemed like the easier option turned out to be more work and not the best idea. The removal process took days, resources, and effort, but it was necessary to build a lasting new deck.

Even though the demolition was necessary, that doesn't mean it was fun or even rewarding in the moment. No matter how difficult the building can be, my husband always comes home with a sense of accomplishment, unless it's demo day. When we see God moving us forward, and when we see beautiful things being built and growing in our lives, we are reassured that we are moving in the right direction. The removal process is not as rewarding. When God begins to take us through the pruning process, we can get discouraged. And while this part isn't the most fun, it is always necessary. Because not everything we've packed in our figurative suitcase is necessary or fitting for our promised land.

When God chose to lead the children of Israel by the way of the wilderness, he wasn't only taking them out of Egypt, but he was taking Egypt out of them. Leaving Egypt as slaves and entering the promised land free would require pruning in the middle. Pruning is a process of trimming, cutting, or removing dead or overgrown branches in order to increase fruitfulness. The purpose of pruning is not to limit or remove growth, but to make growth possible.

While we are in the waiting, it is easy for us to point to our growth as a sign that God is working. In the same way, I have learned more and more to recognize his hand in the pruning too. Now, if you're picturing God in heaven with a massive pair of pruning shears, you're not alone in your imagery. I've pictured it that way too, and it sounds painful and harsh. But God is not in heaven holding a pair of shears bigger than the clouds with the purpose of exposing us or leaving us vulnerable. He is gentle and, in compassion and love for us, is delicately removing things that are no longer producing fruit in our lives. He doesn't take things away but makes room for more. This pruning process is not harmful, but helpful and a necessary process for our growth and change.

> I am the true vine, and my Father is the vinedresser. Every branch in me that does not bear fruit he takes away, and every branch that does bear fruit he prunes, that it may bear more fruit. Already you are clean because of the word that I have spoken to you. Abide in me, and I in you. As the branch cannot bear fruit by itself, unless it abides in the vine, neither can you, unless you abide in me. I am the vine; you are the branches. Whoever abides in me and I in him, he it is that bears much fruit, for apart from me you can do nothing. If anyone does not abide in me he is thrown away like a branch and withers; and the branches are gathered, thrown into the fire, and burned. If you abide in me, and my words abide in you, ask whatever you wish, and it will be done for you. (John 15:1–7)

The year 2016 didn't go the way I planned. To date, it has been one of the most challenging years of my life. I desperately wanted to close my eyes and wish it away. That year, we experienced great loss, betrayal, heartache, and pain. It was a lonely season, a time when God seemed distant and quiet. I have always been a positive person, always looking for the hope in dark situations. But this particular year, it was hard to find. As I would regain my footing, it seemed like another harsh wave would come crashing in, disrupting my balance. I really wanted out.

I remember feeling as though my heart was actually broken. Never before had I been so sad. Never before had I experienced such sorrow. I cried for God's rescue, for his deliverance. And as I did, he met me and asked me, "Sarah, what will you *get out* of this year?" Life can be hard, situations can be difficult, and seasons can be dry. When those times come, our first response is usually to want out. But rather than asking *when* we can get out of it, we should be asking *what* we can get out of it. When we search for what we can learn, understand, and grow from in the midst of our trouble, our pain carries a purpose. There is purpose in our struggle, and there is purpose in our waiting. Yes, God is a deliverer and he will deliver us out of dry and tough seasons, but it's up to us to get something out of it.

So many people wish to forget the passing year, bury it, burn it, and even throw it away, but God doesn't work that way. Although he makes all things new and desires for us to look forward, he builds on what we have experienced, walked through, and even learned from. As much as I wanted to leave 2016 in the dust, I knew I needed to take some things with me. I'm thankful for all that I walked through and experienced that year, the good, the bad, and the ugly. I don't say that because it's over; I say that because in September, while I begged him to get me out, he gave me eyes to see what I could get out of it all. I finished that year so differently. It was a newfound strength. I no longer saw the trials and the setbacks as harsh moments orchestrated by God, but moments when God could use them for my advantage.

Before ringing in the New Year, someone asked me to rate the year on a scale of one to ten. It was impossible for me to score 365 days into one number. If I had to rate it in terms of challenging, I would say close to an eight. If I had to rate it in terms of awesome, I would equally rate it an eight, as one of the best years of my life. The hard stuff helped me discover who I am and what I am made of. It was the uncomfortable moments that ushered in fresh grace, new strength, and greater faith.

I compare it to working out. The best workouts are usually also the most challenging. Even though they are hard, they are awesome all at the same time. It's how I felt about 2016, and that is why days before the New Year, I was actually a little sad to see that year go. It was challenging, but that's what made it equally beautiful. This is why we must remain encouraged even when what we are believing for is delivered in an undesired, challenging package. Trust that God has heard the desires of your heart, is honoring your prayers, and is leading you.

If I looked at all that happened over that year, it wouldn't measure up to be considered a *best year ever* kind of year. Not even close. But when I looked at who I had become and the faithfulness of God in every detail, it ranked up there as one of the best years of my life. If Joseph were asked to rate his years in prison, in a pit, or in slavery, I am not sure he would categorize them as anything but incredible. But if he looked back and recounted the moments that should have crushed him but made him stronger and the moments when he experienced the tangible hand of God in his life, I am sure he would agree that those years were every-thing he hoped for.

When God opens a door, we want to shout about his good-ness, but when he closes a door, we question his goodness. I have never been more grateful for every closed door and unanswered prayer, for every plan that doesn't come to pass, and for every har-vest that has yet to come forth. They have led me to this moment, for such a time as this.

God's plans for us far exceed anything we could ever dream up, hope for, or work toward. He knows all things and is fully aware of every detour, change of direction, or roadblock you might be experiencing. We desire the predictable and feel con-fident in times of peace. Often times, God reveals himself there. However, I have also experienced his presence in the midst of the chaos and in the uncertain moments of my life. When life seems to be turned upside down, when things seem to be removed, and when my control seems to be failing, there is a confident hope that has surfaced. I know that the same God who met me in the peace is in the midst of the movement. When we pray, he hears those prayers with active ears. So don't resist the movement; embrace it. He is just moving the pieces around for your good!

What's Next?

I have been married for more than twelve years; we have three kids and two dogs. Our life is filled to the brim, so I don't get asked as many questions as I used to. When I was finishing high school, the big question was, "Are you going to college?" When I enrolled in the university, the next question was, "What are you going to major in?" As I was graduating with my BA degree, my parents, who paid for my university experience, wanted to know what I was going to do with my life.

When I was single, Grandma Lydia wanted to know if there was a special someone who had my attention. And when I met my husband, my girlfriends wanted to know when we were going to get engaged. Not too long after he popped the question, like five minutes or so after, my sisters wanted to know how long before the wedding. Once we were married, the baby question happened. We had twins, so the questions took a small pause. But once we sang our girls "Happy Birthday," the question was then, "Will you try again?"

We are a culture that is very excited about the next thing. We want to know what is around the corner. If you are anything like me, it is easy to be thinking about tomorrow or maybe even five years from now. I think it's important that we have a vision for our lives, and I believe planning and preparing are good things to do. But we can't live there. There is way too much in the right here and now that deserves our entire attention.

The gift of tomorrow can rob us of our today.

When we choose to fully embrace today and to give our attention to what God is doing right now, I believe we will live less frustrated lives. I believe we will be freer to enjoy and celebrate the tiny, small victories that often seem ordinary and insignificant. The "*If* I could only have this, or get this, or do this, *then* I will finally be happy" is a trap! At first we are excited, feeling on cloud nine, only to find ourselves no longer satisfied, wanting and wishing for more. We will be approaching a waiting season, enduring a waiting season, or experiencing the completion of that waiting season, only to head into a new time of waiting and expecting all over again.

The end of my waiting season wasn't really about accomplishment or destination, status or possession, but an internal work. It's an inner resolve to really know that God is good to me. It is a new perspective to see his work at hand in every season. It is surrendering, trusting his timing, his way. It is a loosened grip of control to my life. It is declaring that he is good, even if I don't see what I am believing for happen. It is embracing an eternal perspective, knowing that everything is working together for a purpose far greater. It is praying as though I have no reason to doubt, trusting like I have never been let down, and believing as though I have never been discouraged. It looks like taking the attention off myself and placing my hope and my pursuit in Jesus.

Waiting can sound like a passive posture, where we aren't doing anything. We picture that college student who is waiting for that perfect job to arrive at his doorstep, while playing video games all day. The actual definition of *waiting* is "the action of staying where one is or delaying action until a particular time or until something else happens." Did you catch that key word *action*? Waiting is active. Waiting is a choice. A choice to remain right where you are, immovable to what might be going on all around you. It is a choice to be unwavering when there is no evidence in sight that God is working on your behalf.

TWELVE

Lose the *Attitude*

Life in the middle has a way of revealing what's buried deep inside of us. When things are going well and when everything is firing on all cylinders, it is easy to show our best. But the days that show who we really are and what we believe are full of delays or moments when we feel like God isn't doing what we want him to do.

Have you ever been on the other side of an apology, after someone has flown off the handle and said something unkind to you? Or perhaps you have lost your cool and said things to someone else that you later regretted? Most people apologize by reassuring the other person that they didn't really mean what they said. But in Scripture, we see that from the abundance of the heart the mouth speaks. That means the words we say come from a place inside of us.

Or maybe you know someone or many someones who always have something to complain about. It can be about anything—the weather, the political climate, their job, their employees, their children, or their spouses. No matter how sunny it is outside, they find something to be unhappy about.

The children of Israel complained about everything. They were habitual complainers who were stuck in a cycle of discontentment, a vicious cycle that would prolong their journey to the promised land. And while God can handle our honesty, our frustrations, our fears, and our uncertainties, petitioning God with our requests is different than complaining. Petitioning God moves us closer to him and expresses our need for him in our lives; it reveals our need for his intervention. Complaining moves us away from God, expressing our confidence in self and our belief that we know better than God.

Whether it's about traffic, our work schedules, our spouse's never-ending demands at home, or the reality that we have to buy a new set of tires when we would much rather go on a family vacation—they all place our personal happiness at the center of the universe. Many of the things we complain about are the result of the things we've prayed for, believed for, and waited on God to do! The taxing work schedule is the result of the promotion we prayed for. And rather than rejoicing in the promotion, we turn our attention to self and highlight the schedule that's keeping us from relaxing on the weekends.

The Israelites did this too. Rather than seeing God's provision of manna from heaven, they complained about no longer having the meat they had in slavery. Rather than rejoicing as they witnessed God part the Red Sea, they focused on the desert and the dry lands. God was doing an incredible work for them, through them, and with them, yet they missed it entirely because they complained.

We miss out when we complain. We stay stuck in situations longer when we use our words to destruct and uproot what God is doing in our lives. Our words are powerful, and we must choose to use them to echo the heart of God, bring life to situations, and advance God's will. Complaining is a habit we must break—no matter how big or small.

But it starts with the heart.

The Greek word translated *complainer* means literally "one who is discontented with his lot in life." It was evident that the Israelites were in a better place physically. They were no longer slaves but free people! But their discontentment was a heart issue that blinded their ability to see God's provision.

One night after a long day, I plopped myself in the bed and before my head hit the pillow, I started sharing every thought, emotion, fear, and frustration with my husband. I was complaining about several things, many of which were out of our control. I complained about the kitchen needing to be cleaned, lunches that needed to be packed, and all of the things that I still had to get done before the next day. I hoped venting and laying it all out there would bring a sense of relief or comfort, but it didn't. I just verbally unloaded so much on my husband, and that wasn't fair. So I apologized and then began listing off the things I was grateful for. I started general, and then I got really specific.

I was thankful for the cup of coffee he served me in bed that morning.

I was thankful for the leaves that were changing colors.

I was thankful for the belly laughs I shared with my kids.

I was thankful for the text I received from him that read, "I love you." Just because. Suddenly, a shift happened in my heart and in my mind. Sure, there were things that I wished could be different, but gratitude ushers in peace and joy.

Worrying or stressing out about our situation wasn't going to change the outcome, but it was going to hinder my present and cloud my ability to see all the great things that were happening! Gratitude is the best attitude, and I believe it is the secret to miracles. When there is opportunity to be overwhelmed, there is also opportunity to express gratitude. It doesn't mean that we are grateful for the situation, but it does mean that we can resist the temptation to be intimidated by our situation, becoming more interested in seeing how God will work it out.

Since then, I try my best to do this as often as possible. I tell my husband the moments when I notice his hard work, his affection toward his kids, the grace he shows me when I had a bad moment. I tell my kids when I notice their kindness or compassion. I send voice texts or pick up the phone to simply tell my friends how important they are to me. And every day, when I'm driving down the road, I find ways to remind God how I see him in the beautiful sunset.

Just like complaining is a habit we develop over time, we can cultivate an attitude of gratitude. No matter how tired I am or how early I have to wake up, beginning my day thanking God for air in my lungs and for another day of life is something I refuse to take for granted! I journal and write down how God has provided or moments that he expressed his love toward me through a person or a situation. As a family, we celebrate every tiny victory, always giving the glory to Jesus first! And when we think we're done celebrating, we celebrate a little more, for a little bit longer. We give God the credit and express our gratitude, knowing that it is all because of him. These habits cultivate a heart of gratitude. These habits keep our hearts overflowing with thankfulness as we look back and remember all that he has done, as we look up to notice what he is doing, and as we look out with expectation of all that he has yet to do!

We retell the stories of his faithfulness. It was our third-year anniversary, and we didn't have enough money to do anything special, so we decided that we would make the most of it instead of being discouraged. Our plan was to order Taco Bell and watch a movie at home. Our anniversary is on a national holiday, so we always have the day off from work. Well, that particular morning, he got called into work at the last minute so he could drive a couple of pastors to the airport. On his way to drop them off and after a great conversation during the car ride (not having shared about our anniversary or lack of money), a pastor slipped him a one hundred dollar bill and said, "Take your wife on a date!" That night, we went out for a yummy dinner and a movie! We were thankful for the generosity of that pastor and his willingness to respond to God's leading. But more than that, we were thankful to God who cares about the details of our lives and who orchestrated the whole thing.

These stories we keep fresh in our minds and share about them as often as we can. These stories encourage our faith. "Every good gift and every perfect gift is from above, coming down from the Father of lights, with whom there is no variation or shadow due to change" (James 1:17). In moments of trial, we have choices to make, and those choices make all the difference. Are we going to simply try to get out of them, or are we going to find the value in them? Are we going to complain about the sacrifices we've made, or are we going to speak life over the seeds we have sown and continue to sow? Are we going to allow offense to grip our hearts, or are we going to allow these moments to teach us how to love, serve, and consider others better?

Maybe you are right in the thick of it and you have plenty of reasons to complain. Perhaps you are discouraged or maybe even a little bitter about your circumstances. I get it. I've been there. Heck, I still find myself there in some moments. And while I'm not suggesting we welcome hard moments with open arms, I am suggesting that we can grow in hard times. Not only can we grow in difficult situations, but we can experience joy!

The enemy of our lives comes to kill, steal, and destroy our lives, yet he has no authority. He cannot take away the seeds of faith we have sown, nor can he undo the steps of obedience we have made when it has seemed crazy. And while he cannot do any of those things, he can try to convince us to! He can get us to curse the seeds of faith we've sown, he can make us regret moments where we expressed generosity, and he can get us to turn away from pressing through and moving forward, step by step. The enemy is powerless, but he who is within you is powerful! What you are going through is there to help grow you! Stay confident, remain faithful, guard your heart, and press on.

Stick It Out!

> But blessed is the man who trusts me, GOD,
>> the woman who sticks with GOD.
> They're like trees replanted in Eden,
>> putting down roots near the rivers—
> Never a worry through the hottest of summers,
>> never dropping a leaf,
> Serene and calm through droughts,
>> bearing fresh fruit every season. (Jer. 17:7–8 MSG)

These verses paint a beautiful picture of what our life can look like in the middle of our waiting. This is a picture of a woman who is not led by her feelings, but instead rooted in her faith. Do you know that girl who is up when things are up and is down when things are down? The girl you don't know what to expect when you ask her how things are going? If we're honest, we've all been that girl. Our Heavenly Father has crafted us with emotions. Our emotions tell a lot about where our trust is hidden and reflect what we believe. Our emotions should never be our guide. When we worry, our emotions are telling us that we are not fully trusting. When we run away in fear, our emotions are letting us know that we have not fully surrendered. I don't want to be that girl who is riding the roller coaster of emotions. I want to be more like the woman described here. Serene and calm through the driest droughts.

One year, while I was speaking at a women's conference, one of my friends was in the audience. I was speaking about this topic of navigating the middle and encouraging every girl in the room not to give up on her promise. I knew her story and what she had been waiting on for many years. I had spent time praying with her during these difficult years and had many moments invested in her story. She and I hadn't seen each other in some time and didn't have a chance to talk before the conference. So, when I scanned the crowd and noticed her, I was so excited to see her there. During my talk, I kept locking eyes with her. Her gaze was different and her posture was sure. Everything about her demeanor reflected a girl who was on the other side of her waiting. Her response told the story of a girl who had seen the promise fulfilled in her life. She nodded with a confident yes anytime I mentioned the faithfulness of God and smiled when I commented that God was a promise keeper and a truth teller. When we finally got a chance to speak, she let me know that she in fact was experiencing her miracle moment.

My heart leaped with great joy in excitement! We hugged and hugged some more and shed a few tears together, rejoicing in the news she shared with me. My friend is a strong and courageous gal. She loves the Lord, serves him passionately, and always has a smile on her face. She navigated her season of waiting with strength. But I will forever remember the statement her entire countenance made without uttering a single word.

Her posture reflected the woman described in Jeremiah 7.

Picture yourself on the other side of your waiting season—the faith you possess, the assurance you feel, and the peace you rest in. All of it. Those emotions aren't only available there, but they are available for you right in the middle. Take hold of that right here and now. The God of the promise is the God in the middle. He is the God in the midst of the dry and barren land, and he is the God of the harvest. He is the God in the middle of the drought, and he is the God of the provision. Bearing fresh fruit means our desert season doesn't have to be dry. But it can be filled with new life as we wait. Bearing fruit means cultivating growth in our life; it's surrendering to the planting, pruning, watering, and harvesting.

Weeks later, we got sad news: her miracle moment took a turn. I was heartbroken. As I prayed and cried out to God on her behalf, a gentle voice whispered to my shattered heart and gave me a message of love to share with my friend who was hurting so deeply. I believe he has given me the same message of love to share with you, as you are experiencing the highs and lows of your waiting season.

Maybe you are desiring to adopt, and just when you think you are going to adopt a child you have loved and cared for, you get a call that a family member wants custody of that child. In one moment, you find yourself filled with faith and rejoicing, and in the next, you are utterly heartbroken.

Or maybe you have a sickness and you have experienced great strides toward your healing. Things have looked like they were getting better, and suddenly your health takes a turn for the worse. In one moment, you are declaring that God is your Healer, and in the next you are feeling so confused as to why you are not healed yet.

Perhaps you believed you finally found the person for you. You have prayed and waited patiently for God to send the right person into your life. You are excited for your journey ahead, and suddenly the relationship ends, and the person you thought was for you turns out not to love you back. Or they turn out not to be the person you thought they were. You are single again, filled with sadness. Minutes ago, you were declaring that God knows best for you, then here you are feeling like you have wasted time and are further than ever from your promise.

Maybe you are believing for your spouse to give his life to Jesus. You just finished texting your friends about the meaningful conversation you had with him about faith, and you are seeing his heart change right before your eyes. And no sooner than you hit the send button, it looks like he is walking in the opposite direction. His actions and even his attitude toward you have shifted. His walls are back up and the comments he used to make are back. It looks like you are back to square one.

I don't know why things happen the way they do. I don't know why healing takes time or why relationships end. I don't know why people aren't able to start a family when they want to. But what I do know is that God does. I don't like using the cliché "Everything happens for a reason." That line feels empty, lacking substance. But I do believe that God is a good God who can be trusted. A God who works all things together for our good.

Blessed is the woman who sticks with God! He has you, he is with you, and he went to great measures to stick with you. When he sent his Son to die on a cross while we were still in our mess, he showed us just how real his love for us is. If he is the same God who would go to such great lengths to display his love and affection toward us, why would he not orchestrate anything less than beautiful for you?

We don't stand secure because we are naive and denying the reality of our situations. But we stand secure in the finished work that Jesus already did for us. He is the same God yesterday, today, and forever. He knows our beginnings, and he knows the end. So he is trustworthy in every moment in between. Some might say that our faith is imagination or a denial of reality. But faith is not passive or imagined. It is a deep belief that what we desire not only could happen but that it will. Faith is acting on what you believe to be true, about God and about your situation.

I know it's painful to wait. I know it's hard to see how this downward turn can actually be of value for what you are believing God to work out for you.

THIRTEEN

Frustrating *Faith*

*J*esus's friends Mary and Martha understood the many turns of waiting too.

We read in John about a guy named Lazarus who was ill. Lazarus wasn't just any ordinary guy; he was a really great friend of Jesus and the brother of Mary and Martha. Like any sisters would, Mary and Martha sent word to their close friend Jesus about Lazarus's illness. They knew his love for them and for their brother, so they were certain that if Jesus knew they were in need, he would do whatever he could to be there. Their belief in Jesus was so strong, so secure—not only that he would come but that he would come in time to heal their brother. Mary, Martha, and Lazarus had all experienced firsthand the miraculous works of Jesus. They had spent time with him, broken bread with him, and trusted him with their lives—and now they requested Jesus to come quickly.

But that is not what happened. Scripture tells us that Jesus loved Martha, Mary, and Lazarus *so* he decided to make them wait longer. No, he didn't drop what he was doing and rush to where Lazarus was, but he chose to stay where he was. When Jesus finally arrived on the scene, his friend was already dead and had been in the tomb for four days. Studies show that the fourth day is when bodies began to decay, and no signs of life or hope remain. When Jesus arrived, it had been many days since he was first made aware of Lazarus's situation. Days when Jesus could have intervened, could have shown up, but he didn't.

Martha and Mary believed in the power of Jesus and knew that if he got word that their brother was in trouble, surely he would come to their rescue. They not only believed that Jesus would come, but we see how Martha also believed that had Jesus come in time, it would have ended differently. Jesus was their friend and someone with whom they spent time. If there were friends who were deserving of his rescue and his attention, it was them.

Betrayed, abandoned, confused. These are only a few of the many emotions I am sure they experienced. I wonder if Lazarus asked for Jesus after they had sent word, wondering where he was or how long they thought it would be before he was coming. I wonder if Lazarus experienced sadness. Here he was experiencing the worst season of his life, and his best friend was nowhere to be found. His sisters were left carrying the weight of watching their brother die. And then he died, and Jesus still wasn't there. People from all over journeyed to say their goodbyes and offer their condolences—and still no Jesus.

They made preparations for his burial. They carried the weight of the arrangements and every detail to honor the life of their brother. And still no Jesus. I wonder if they questioned

Jesus's love for them. I think I would have. Looking back at my life, when Jesus didn't respond in the time frame I thought he should have, it caused me to question his love. Preparing a funeral is a lot of work, with a lot of details. In biblical times, it was no different. It was hard, it was sad, and it was painful. They were exhausted mentally, physically, and spiritually.

And then Jesus showed up.

Jesus, I can think of at least twenty-seven different moments when you could have arrived on the scene. Seventy-two of them happened before Lazarus died. You might know the end of this story, and you are assuring me that this ending is way cooler. But let's sit right in this moment and pretend we don't know how this story is going to end. In fact, this seems to be the end of the story— Jesus loves Lazarus, Jesus hears about his sickness, Jesus chooses not to come, Lazarus dies, Lazarus is buried, Jesus comes. The end.

Sometimes I think I write the better stories. In my prayers, I include, "Hey, Jesus, this is a perfect time for a huge miracle. If you do this right now, everyone will see just how great you are!" Martha expressed the same feeling. She and Mary believed that Jesus was Healer, so their ideal outcome included Jesus healing Lazarus. Even the other Jews who were present, those who had gathered around Lazarus's family, questioned: "Could not he who opened the eyes of the blind man also have kept this man from dying?"

I'm sure you have people in your world who are looking in at your not-so-ideal situation. They know you serve God and trust him, and yet he doesn't seem to be fixing your situation. He doesn't seem to be moving you through the middle any faster. They might be asking how a God who loves you could allow this to happen. If my kids were in danger or if they needed me, I would do everything in my power to rescue them or change their situation. That is what you do when someone you care about is in need of help. So not only was this situation disheartening for Mary and Martha, but it was confusing for those looking in. I am sure people were wondering how this was all going to work out for them, and they were taking notice of how Mary and Martha were managing this tension.

Jesus finally arrived, and Martha ran out to greet him. When she made her way to him, it was not with clenched fists blaming Jesus for the outcome. She reminded Jesus that he could have done something to prevent this. In the midst of her great suffering and having waited a long time for Jesus, she still believed that Jesus could petition God. I don't know who all was around to see this encounter take place, but if I were an outsider looking in and had the chance to witness my friend Martha pursue Jesus in spite of his distance and his actions, I would take notice. Jesus could have healed her brother. But a greater work was taking place here.

Jesus uttered five powerful words, asking her, "Did I not tell you?" He brought the greater work into focus: Jesus was not only Healer but he was the Resurrection. Jesus entrusted Mary and Martha with this story of both tragedy and triumph, a story that would change their understanding of Jesus. This moment would move their understanding from a Jesus who changes things to a Jesus who would change *everything*. The death of Jesus revealed that he was not only someone who could heal but that he also had the power and victory over all things, including death itself.

And when he went to the cross, Jesus *changed* everything. When our situations seem to be at a standstill and Jesus doesn't seem to be changing them, we can declare that "Jesus has already changed everything!" Is it easy? No. When healing doesn't come or when the answer is delayed, it is not easy! It's painfully hard. I think it would be easier sometimes if we didn't share the belief that our God is all-powerful. Maybe it would have been easier for Martha too. If she didn't believe that Jesus had the power or the authority to do something about it, maybe it might have been less personal and more just a part of life. And while it doesn't mean that our understanding extinguishes the pain, it does mean that it doesn't defeat us or have the final say.

Some of us are living in offense. Some of us are mad at God for not coming sooner, for not responding the way we desperately believed that he would. This offense is suffocating our faith and polluting our hearts. We have believed the lie that God is out to get us or that somehow he is indifferent to our heart's cry. And while I don't know why this has happened to you—the loss, the tragedy, the suffering, the waiting—do know that God has entrusted you with it. God has given you this story, a story of both tragedy and triumph. For some, the triumph is in the restoration, or in the healing, or in the desired outcome; and for some, the triumph is that even in the loss, the pain, the hardship, we, like Mary, run to Jesus believing that nothing, absolutely nothing, will be wasted. That he will use every broken piece of our story.

When the enemy or naysayers try to fill your heart with bitterness toward God, or when you are tempted to put up walls around your heart, afraid to be let down by God again, remind yourself of this: Jesus, the King of kings, has already done the finished work. When he went to the cross and when he defeated death, he disarmed the power of sickness, loneliness, betrayal, pain, hurt, barrenness, sorrow, and death. And even when it looks like he didn't come soon enough or when it seems like it's the end of the story, run to him again and again!

FOURTEEN

Trust, *Again*

*B*elieve like you've never been let down. Trust like you've never been disappointed. Pray like you've never lived to experience moments when things didn't happen the way you hoped they would.

It takes a lot of courage to trust again, to believe again, and to pray again. When you find yourself weary and hesitant, with your guards up around your heart, when past experiences of let-down seem to suffocate the faith you once had, look back. When you look back, you will see that although life has been hard and it may not have always gone the way you wanted it to go, God has been faithful.

In 2010, I found out that my husband and I were expecting our first child. I can remember it as if it were yesterday, me sitting in front of my husband, holding a pregnancy test, making sure I did in fact see two lines. It was so surreal and so incredible. All

I could do was laugh. I had always seen it on movies, when the couple finds out they are expecting, and I had seen my friends and family experience this moment; but this time it was me. So many questions filled my mind: Are we ready for this? Are we old enough to have a baby? Is this going to forever change our lives? Are our parents going to freak out? For what seemed like forever, BJ and I sat in our living room and smiled, cried, and kept pinching ourselves because what we had just found out didn't seem real. We prayed that God would watch over my body and that "no weapon formed against us would prosper." We knew that this baby was so much more than just a child; it was a promise from God.

We wanted to tell our family first, so we had to go back to work and pretend that nothing life-changing had just happened. I, of course, immediately got online and began to read all about what was happening in my body, how big the baby was, and on and on. It was so much fun looking at all that was happening inside my body. BJ and I were ecstatic! A few days later, I experienced some spotting, and a huge wave of fear came over me. I immediately told BJ what was going on. I knew something wasn't right. When I told him what was happening, we both decided we were not going to jump to any conclusions because we didn't want to start this pregnancy off in fear. I continued to pray and believe for the very best. I have always had strong faith in God; and at the time, I wasn't someone who was very fearful. I started experiencing severe pain, and we decided to go to the emergency room.

It was like a really bad dream that I couldn't get out of. Doctors and nurses came in and out of the room where I was, drawing blood, running tests; they all said something was wrong without saying anything. The whole time, we prayed and declared God's Word over me and the baby. There wasn't a doubt in my mind that everything was going to be okay. The doctor came in and told us that I was going to have to go into emergency surgery because the baby was no longer alive inside my body. The doctors needed to act fast and perform an emergency surgery to prevent any further damage. What I learned then was that ectopic pregnancies are life-threatening.

I looked at BJ and told him to call every person we knew to pray! As the doctors left us alone for a few minutes, we prayed like we had never prayed before and had no doubt everything was going to work out. In a matter of moments, I was ready and prepped for surgery. It was so scary. I had never gone to the hospital for anything, never had an IV, so all of what was happening was so overwhelming. BJ called our family and friends to let them know what was happening. In one breath, he announced that we were pregnant, and in the next, he told them why he was calling. A few of my friends and my pastor met me in the room before I was sent in for surgery. We prayed and believed God for the miraculous.

About an hour later, I was coming out of surgery, and I asked the doctor what happened. He told me that it was in fact an ectopic pregnancy and that they had to remove the baby. The first thing that came out of my mouth was, "I don't understand." As I uttered those words, still in a bit of a slumber, I was reminded of a morning a few months before when I was awakened out of sleep.

I couldn't go back to sleep and felt inclined to pray. I fumbled my way downstairs, made myself a cup of coffee, and started washing the dishes. I guess I felt if I was going to be awake at this hour of the day, I'd better make it productive. As I washed the dishes with one eye open, I started to repeat this phrase over and over: "Lord, I trust you." It's all I said for the next ten minutes. I didn't know what was happening around me or what the next few weeks would hold for us, but I knew there was an assurance that

I needed to possess. Every time I said that phrase, I became more and more sure of what I was declaring.

And as I was being taken out of the operating room, I heard the Holy Spirit ask me, "Sarah, do you trust me?" From the depths of my broken heart, I responded with, "Lord, I trust you. Lord, I trust you." It didn't make sense, nor did I really want to say that I trusted God, but deep within me, I did.

It was the hardest thing I had ever been through and one of the most challenging times of my life. The days to come were difficult, as I was not only healing physically but also mentally and spiritually. I had moments when I was okay and then moments when I would just cry. Our friends and family, our pastors, and our church family rallied behind us and were there for us every step of the way. They encouraged us and believed with us that all things were going to work out for our good.

I remember one conversation in particular that I had with one of my friends, and we got on the topic of Job. We were talking about how Job went through so much trial and that he lost everything, but God gave him double. I had heard this story many times, and I usually talked about it when someone was going through a tough time. We so often use it to encourage people that God is faithful and that he will give us more! But at that time, I saw this story so differently. I asked my friend, "What if Job didn't want double, but he just wanted what he had?" What was so significant about God giving Job double and not so significant about him just letting him have what he had? What was the purpose of allowing what had happened to us to take place? I knew that God was able to prevent what happened to us, but he allowed it.

Perhaps you too have experienced loss. And you just want what you had.

So why does God allow us to go through hard times? Why does he allow pain, hurt, disappointment to be a part of our lives? Why does he allow bad things to happen to good people? I know that I am not the only person who has asked these questions. There have been many times in my life when things just didn't make sense to me. I didn't understand why things were happening to me or to the people I love and care about. This time, it was no different to me. Why did God allow me and BJ to lose our first baby? Why didn't he step in and heal me? Wouldn't that make more sense?

It was a few days after the surgery, and I was lying down in my bed and was led to this verse: "And we know that for those who love God all things work together for good, for those who are called according to his purpose" (Rom. 8:28). In all things, God works. In all things, God works. That means in the good times, he works. In the bad times, he works. In all things, God works.

The Bible is filled with dedicated, God-fearing people who accomplished great things for the kingdom of God. In every story, we see uncertainty, times of trial, times of pain, and times of waiting. In this life, we are going to face things that do not seem fair, and when we give our lives over to God, it does not exempt us from such pain or tragedy. When we surrender our lives to God, we are simply giving him the power and the ability to work on our behalf. "I have said these things to you, that in me you may have peace. In the world you will have tribulation. But take heart; I have overcome the world" (John 16:33).

No, it doesn't always make sense, but it does always work out for our good. Trials draw us nearer to God. They teach us, mold us, shape us, and prepare us for the life God has for us. I don't remember a time in my life when I have learned something or advanced in my life when things were going well. It has been in the times of pain and disappointment when I grew stronger and wiser. The enemy puts tragedy into our lives and hopes to steal, kill, and destroy us, but when we stand on God's Word and his promises, such as that "he will never leave us nor forsake us," we guarantee victory! No matter the outcome, no matter the results, God works! He is sovereign and is able to do the impossible. Every time we walk through tough situations, we are stronger and more able to face what lies in front of us.

If only the enemy knew that you were going to be stronger, wiser, greater, and more equipped after you had been tried, I don't think he would continue to challenge and attack the children of God. God allows things to happen to us because he has faith in us. We have been made in the image of God, and "no weapon formed against us will prosper." God wants to do the miraculous in each of us, but miracles are birthed out of tragedy and uncertain situations. I knew that God was going to get the final say in my situation; I knew that he was going to do the miraculous. I just didn't know it was going to be a few months later with twins!

Whatever it is that you are going through or have gone through or are about to go through, know that in all things, God works! James 1 says this: "Consider it a sheer gift, friends, when tests and challenges come at you from all sides. You know that under pressure, your faith-life is forced into the open and shows its true colors. So don't try to get out of anything prematurely. Let it do its work so you become mature and well-developed, not deficient in any way" (James 1:2–4 MSG).

God's desire is for us to be victorious! He is for you! He is for me!

Made for This

Were things falling apart when there was a hungry crowd of five thousand with no pizza buffet to feed them? Or were they falling into place when through that moment Jesus and his disciples performed one of the most incredible miracles?

When we are led by our emotions, we will ride the worst roller coaster of our lives. In one moment we are like, "Oh no!" and then the next moment we are like, "Oh yeah!" Our emotions are fickle, and our emotions can't be trusted to lead us as we journey through our lives. Our emotions will cloud our judgment and keep us from seeing the full story. So many of us desire to be used by God in a feeding of the five thousand kind of way. We pray audaciously and put it all on the line, and then the moment things don't look like they are going right for us, we want to jump ship. Following Jesus will take you from a mountaintop, miracle experience to right in the middle of the storm.

Imagine being one of the disciples—you just saw a little boy's lunch feed an army of hangry people. One by one, you saw food being multiplied, so much that you and your friends had leftovers. The adrenaline, the excitement, the awestruck wonder of Jesus and all that he is able to do fueled your faith in an exciting way! You are high-fiving each other, fist bumping, taking selfies with the leftover basket, and posting it all over social media. You are declaring the power of Jesus and declaring the miracle worker that he is.

And then you and your friends get in a boat. Perhaps you are still reflecting on all that just transpired, or maybe you are already looking ahead for bigger and better. Either way, what you just experienced was life-changing, history-making. It just went viral on YouTube. No doubt they thought to themselves, "We were made for this!"

Immediately after that, Jesus purposefully sent them right into the middle of a storm. The storm was raging so violently that the disciples thought they were going to die. Five seconds ago, they were pouring Gatorade on each other and celebrating their victory moment, and now they are scared for their lives. Can you relate? I know I can. I can relate to every part of it. You witness God do incredible things in your midst, and before you can catch your breath, you are in the middle of a raging storm. This is why we can't allow our emotions to get the best of us, but in all things, remain grounded in the truth about Jesus.

Jesus knowingly sent his disciples into a storm, but he did not send them to die. I am sure they questioned his motives and intentions, and I am sure they felt like Jesus had abandoned them. But Jesus wanted to reveal to his disciples that he was not only the One who could multiply when there is lack. He was also the One who could tell the roaring sea to be still. And just like they believed they were made for that miracle moment as they distributed the loaves and fishes, they were made for this too.

But that wasn't their first response. They weren't ordering their super cool T-shirts with the words *Made for This* to wear during the next miracle. In fact, when Jesus did finally come, they thought he was a ghost and started crying. Their first response was fear, not faith, and it didn't allow them to see it as an opportunity for Jesus to yet again reveal himself to them. They didn't see this as a setup for God's glory to be revealed.

We know Peter as the disciple who walked on water, but we often omit the whole "it took place in the middle of a raging storm" part. So imagine this—the winds and the waves are so intense you are thinking this is the end for you, and Jesus is nowhere in sight. Time passes by, and every moment it gets darker and darker. You're thinking, "Where is this Jesus, and why has he allowed me to experience this?" Then you are pretty sure you are now being greeted by a ghost. And in the midst of it all, your crazy friend Peter decides to talk to this ghost and ask this ghost to call him to walk on the water. Peter walks on water while you're holding on for dear life.

Every moment feels like a decade, and you are afraid.

Right in the middle of your storm, in the darkest moment, someone in your boat experiences a *Made for This* moment. The storm doesn't cease until after Peter and Jesus have their moment together on the water and step back into the boat. And when everything finally calms down, everyone in the boat declares that truly Jesus is the Son of God. Jesus had been saying that, but this revelation was ushered in and made true in their hearts by a raging storm.

The word *immediately* is found multiple times in this passage. It says that *immediately* after the feeding of the five thousand, Jesus sends his disciples in the boat. And when Peter begins to sink, Jesus rescues him *immediately*. There will be things in your life that Jesus does immediately. I pray that if you are sick in body right now, Jesus will heal you immediately. I pray that if you are asking the Lord for a child, he will give you a baby immediately. I stand with you believing that God can do things, immediately!

But sometimes, he doesn't answer immediately. Jesus didn't immediately rescue the disciples from the storm; and even when he physically arrived, he didn't immediately tell the storm to cease. He allowed the disciples to wait. It doesn't feel good when he allows us to wait, when it feels like he isn't coming to our rescue. But I have heard it before and I will mention it here, God is still moving in our waiting.

Let's *Go!*

*A*s I have compiled my writings, I have read about bad days that I experienced, and some were really heartbreaking days. Days when words were filled with frustration, doubt, heartache, and pain. Some days were good days, and I shared about a fun new thing one of my kids was up to, or the light that I found at the end of the tunnel. The days when I experienced a miracle from heaven. As different as each day has been, and no matter the time frame or span of years these entries come from, there was something so familiar, so identical about all of them collectively. Every single worry or doubt seemed to have worked itself out in the pages to come.

As I have sat in my room, in a coffee shop, or in my makeshift home office, reading and almost reliving these moments, tears of gratitude have streamed down my face. I just finished reading about the time my girls were born and the many fears I had as a new mom. The uncertainty in my words is as real right now as it was years ago. Someone in our life at the time promised that he would supply us with diapers for an entire year. Having two little bums to cover, that was one of the best things ever. Until it was time for us to need diapers and our friend was no longer able to come through on his promise. In my journal, I wrote, "God, if he can't make true on his promise, we need you to." I thought that was pretty bold! And as I turn the page, I see that I had written, "BJ just got home with bags of free diapers he got from our diaper depot at church." I think it's safe to say that God showed off for us right then.

I have been disappointed, I have been let down, I have had situations not work out; but as I sit here desperately seeking God about what he would have me write on the final pages of this book, I realize once again that everything I have ever worried about or waited on God for, God has come through for me. Over and over again. Usually not in my timing and almost never completely like I had planned it, but he has taken care of me every step of the way.

And because our memories are fleeting and hard moments hover like a cloud, making it almost impossible to see his hand, let me remind you once again that he is faithful. Look back over the course of your life, and you will see it—that he was faithful, that he is still faithful. His faithfulness will give you courage to believe that he always will be faithful. Believe him to be a truth teller and promise keeper. He will never let you down, because he is a good God who is good to you!

Acknowledgments

Mom and Dad, you two have been my greatest encouragers of every daring and audacious dream. Thank you for championing my voice, ever since I was a little girl. You were always giving me the courage to speak up, write, lead authentically, and be true to who God has fashioned me to be. There's never been a single day or moment when I didn't feel loved and cared for by the both of you, and for that I am grateful. I love you.

BJ, life with you is one wild adventure! Thank you for making me laugh when moments are tough, for reminding me of God's promises when the wait has gotten the best of me, and for leading us with strength, humility, and passion. When I share my dreams with you, you always respond with, "I think that's awesome. How can I help?" When I share my fears with you, you always respond with love. You are the protector of my heart, the leader of our home, and the love of my life, and you're really great at it. Thank you for gifting me the iPad with a note that said, "Go and write your book." You see my victories as our victories, and you show up for me and for our families in too many ways to note. Your belief in people challenges me to keep my heart wide open to people and to God's work. Thank you for all of it.

To my children, Kennedi, Brooklyn, and Jett, you are my greatest purpose on earth. Being your mom is my highest honor. You three have sacrificed so much over the years as the Johnson Crew has chased after God! In every season, you adjust, adapt, and thrive with such grace. Getting the opportunity to see life, experience faith, and love people through your eyes is the greatest gift. Thank you for your understanding when bringing this message of hope to others has meant time away from you. Your shared excitement for this book and for the life God has called us to makes every day so much fun! I love you with all my heart.

To my brothers and sisters, my grandparents, my big family near and far, there's never been a day when I have felt alone, knowing the tribe and support I have in each of you individually and collectively as a family! Thank you for loving me well.

To my mother-in-law, Beth, thank you for raising my favorite person and for loving me like your own daughter. You've been in my corner since day one! Thank you for reading every single word of my manuscript before I hit the send button to my editors. That meant the world to me. I love sharing life with you!

To my best friend Alyssa, anyone who knows you loves you because of your unique gift to love people intentionally. I'm so thankful I've had you by my side at every twist and turn in life. We've shared many conversations about life, and I cherish every single one of them. We have prayed many prayers and have believed God for miracles, so many of which we've seen him answer. Some people go a lifetime without a friend like you, and I'm so glad I didn't have to.

To my cousin Monica, who told me I had a story to tell and that I should consider blogging many years ago. At the time, I thought blogging was for the experts or for those who had it all together, but you reminded me that the story God has entrusted me with should be told. So I posted my first blog over a decade ago, and now look where we are. Thank you for inviting me to church when I was lost. The way I saw you live your life up close opened my heart to Jesus. Your invitation for me to stay at your house and go with you and your family to church the next day marked the day I experienced new life and began this journey with Jesus.

Leafwood Publishers, thank you for believing in me and taking a chance on a first-time author. Thank you for believing in this message and for helping me tell this story. I'll cherish this chapter of my story forever.

To every woman who has prayed for me, cheered me on, and shown up for me, thank you for allowing me to unapologetically run my race. You inspire me by the way you love God, serve his people, and lead your families. I'm better because I'm in this with you.

To Jesus, thank you for saving me and rescuing me. The understanding that I'm fully known and fully loved by you still takes my breath away. I'll spend every day of my life telling everyone about you.